HISTORIC
WARPLANES

BY STEVE MACDONALD

CHARTWELL
BOOKS, INC.

A QUINTET BOOK

ISBN: 0-7858-0337-8

This book was designed and produced by
Quintet Publishing Limited
6, Blundell Street
London N7 9BH

Creative Director: Terry Jeavons
Designer: Wayne Blades
Project Editor: Lindsay Porter
Editor: Peter Arnold
Picture Researcher: Steve McDonald
Revamped By: Nik Morley

Typeset in Great Britain by
Central Southern Typesetters, Eastbourne
Manufactured in China by
Regent Publishing Services Limited.

This edition produced for sale in the USA,
its territories and dependencies only.

Published by Chartwell Books
A Division of Book Sales, Inc.
P.O. Box 7100
Edison, New Jersey 08818–7100

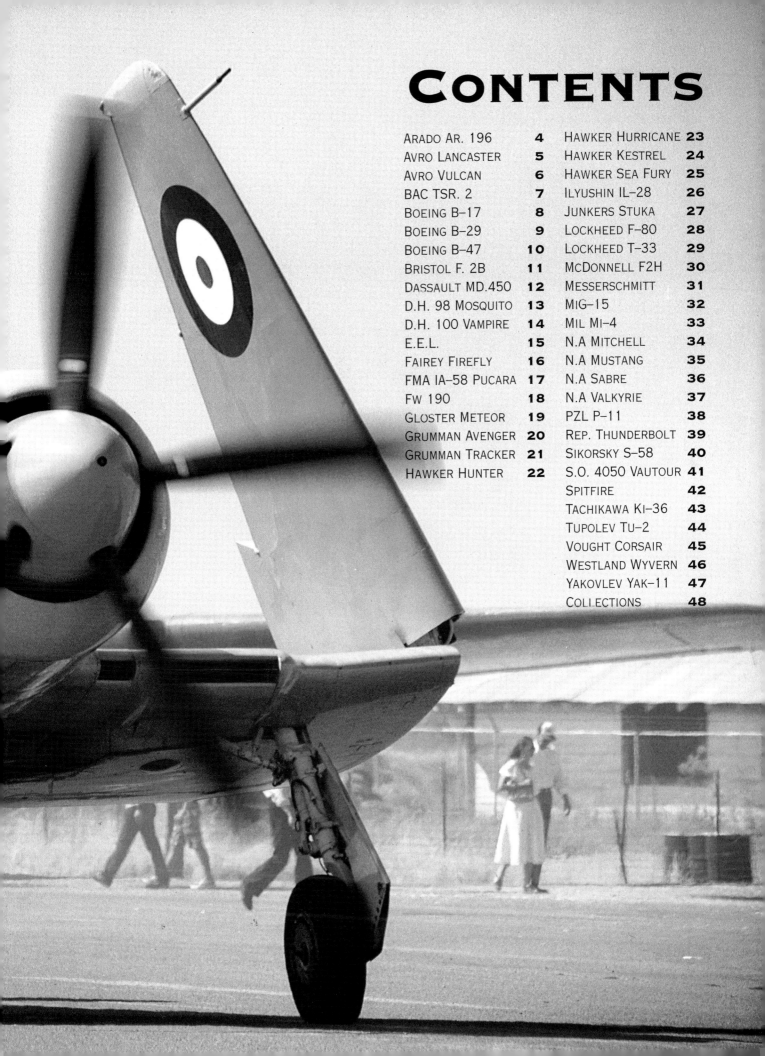

CONTENTS

ARADO AR. 196

OWNER/OPERATOR	:	United States Navy
ADDRESS	:	Willow Grove Naval Air Station, Willow Grove, Pennsylvania 19090, USA
LOCATION	:	15 miles (24 km) north of Philadelphia. Road – Route 611
ADMISSION	:	Exhibits on display alongside boundary fence
FURTHER INFO	:	The airfield is an important US Navy and Marine reserve base.

Below: The Kawanishi NI KI can also be seen at the Wings of Freedom Air and Space Museum.

The most unusual aircraft can often be found where least expected. The US Naval Air Station at Willow Grove, Pennsylvania, offers many gems in its 'Wings of Freedom' collection, including a Japanese World War II Kawanishi N1K1 Shiden 'George' floatplane, complete with genuine bullet holes! The collection's unusual Messerschmitt Me262B-1A – a dual-control training version of Germany's second and most successful jet aircraft of World War II – keeps company with a rare beast, an Italian-built Arado Ar.196A-3 twin-float reconnaissance aircraft.

Probably the most successful seaplane operated by the German Navy's air forces during World War II, the Ar.196 was also used for light bombing and submarine hunting; two of these aircraft were instrumental in the capture of the British submarine HMS *Seal*. The Ar.196 warrants an entry in the record books if only because, as a warship-based aircraft, it took part in every naval operation of the war. In addition to its use on capital ships it became just as important in a coastal-based role.

Of 526 built, GA+DX is one of only three known survivors. Used as a spotter aircraft aboard the infamous German cruiser *Prince Eugen* during its raiding trips, the aircraft was captured intact aboard the ship and taken to Philadelphia as war spoils.

ARADO Ar.196A-3	
COUNTRY OF ORIGIN	**RANGE**
Germany	665 miles (1,070 km)
ENGINES	**CEILING**
one BMW 132K air-cooled radial	22,960 ft (7,000 m)
CREW	**LENGTH**
two	36 ft 1 in (11.00 m)
MAX SPEED	**SPAN**
193 mph (210 km/h)	40 ft 8 in (12.40 m)
	HEIGHT
	14 ft 7 in (4.45 m)

AVRO 683 LANCASTER

Out of the failure of the Avro Manchester bomber came the outstanding success of the Lancaster, arguably the greatest bomber of World War II. A twin-engined design, the Manchester suffered from development problems with its Rolls-Royce Vulture engines. The foresight of Avro's chief designer, Roy Chadwick, led to a developed airframe which would be powered by four Rolls-Royce Merlins – at that time in short supply, as it powered the Spitfire and Hurricane fighters. The redesigned aircraft was an immediate success and 7,377 machines were produced between October 1941 and the end of production in 1946, including 403 built by Victory Aircraft in Canada.

An initial bomb load of 4,000 lb (1,818 kg) increased through development and culminated with the famous 22,000 lb (1,000 kg) Grand Slam bomb designed by Barnes Wallis for destroying Germany's U-boat pens. The most famous operation involving Lancasters was by 617 (Dam Busters) Squadron RAF when they attacked three German dams in May 1943 with devastating effect.

Although not quite the hardest-working example of the type, R5868 survived 137 missions over enemy territory. Allocated to 83 Squadron, RAF with the code OL-Q, it made its first 'Op' on 8 July 1942 and survived the war to end its flying days with 467 (RAF) Squadron on 23 April 1945.

ROYAL AIR FORCE MUSEUM COLLECTION BOMBER COMMAND MUSEUM	
OWNER/OPERATOR :	Royal Air Force
ADDRESS :	Hendon, London NW9 5LL
LOCATION :	9 miles northwest of London. Road – near to the A5
ADMISSION :	Monday-Saturday 1000-1800, Sunday 1400-1800
FURTHER INFO :	The historic aerodrome of Hendon is also the site of the Royal Air Force Museum and the Battle of Britain Museum.

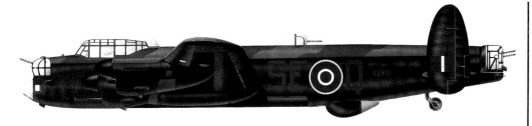

AVRO 683 LANCASTER I
COUNTRY OF ORIGIN
UK
ENGINES
four 1,460 hp Rolls-Royce Merlin XX air-cooled inline
CREW
Seven
MAX SPEED
287 mph (462 km/h)
RANGE
1,660 miles (2,675 km)
CEILING
24,500 ft (7,500 m)
LENGTH
69 ft 6 in (21.18 m)
SPAN
102 ft 0 in (31.09 m)
HEIGHT
20 ft 0 in (6.10 m)

AVRO 698 VULCAN

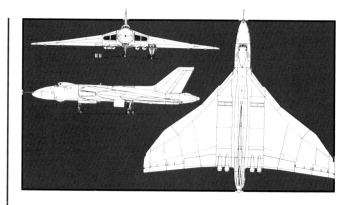

In the twilight years of their life, 26 years after the type entered service with the Royal Air Force, Avro Vulcans bombed the Falkland Islands airport of Port Stanley, so recording the first aggressive use of the aircraft in their long career.

The Vulcan was one of the three strategic 'V' bombers, ordered by the Royal Air Force in the immediate postwar years, as Britain's airborne nuclear deterrent, alongside the earlier Vickers Valiant and the Handley Page Victor. Initially designed to operate at high altitude, it carried the Blue Steel 'stand off' nuclear bomb. The Vulcan was later modified to undertake a tactical low-level role which it achieved with similar success.

The Vulcan is unmistakable owing to its unique delta wing, tested on a series of special development aircraft, also built by Avro. Its superb flight characteristics were enhanced by progressive improvements to the wing design, structural improvements and more powerful engines.

In their initial high-level role, all three 'V' bombers (so called because they each had a swept-back wing leading edge) were painted in an all-white 'anti-flash' colour scheme. The Vulcans later appeared in various camouflage schemes as they adopted new roles, and the few remaining aircraft from the production run of about 100 are displayed in their later colours.

The sole exception is XM603 which was acquired by a group of enthusiasts from the factory at Woodford, Manchester where it was originally built. Some of the group worked on the original airframe. Although not available for public display, except during the annual Royal Air Forces Association air display when the factory gates are thrown open, the aircraft was to have been restored to flying condition. This will not now happen, but XM603 will remain as a memorial to a superb design.

BRITISH AEROSPACE PLC

OWNER/OPERATOR	:	British Aerospace Avro Aircraft Restoration Society
ADDRESS	:	Woodford, Cheshire, UK
LOCATION	:	10 miles (16 km) south of Manchester city centre
ADMISSION	:	Not on public view, except during Woodford Air Show
FURTHER INFO	:	Contact Harry Holmes, British Aerospace PLC, Woodford, Cheshire SK7 1AR.

Below: The Avro Vulcan is also on display at the Strategic Air Command Museum in Nebraska.

AVRO VULCAN B.2		
COUNTRY OF ORIGIN	**RANGE**	
UK	4,000 miles (6,440 km)	
ENGINES	**CEILING**	
four 20,000 lb st (9,072 kg s t) Bristol Siddeley Olympus 201 turbojets	60,000 ft (18,290 m)	
	LENGTH	
CREW	99 ft 11 in (30.45 m)	
five	**SPAN**	
MAX SPEED	111 ft 0 in (33.83 m)	
635 mph (1,016 kph) (Mach 0.96 at 40,000 ft (12,400 m))	**HEIGHT**	
	27 ft 2 in (8.28 m)	

BRITISH AIRCRAFT CORPORATION TSR. 2

Many aircraft projects have been killed off at birth through political expediency, economic pressure or misguided advice. The Avro Canada Arrow Interceptor was one such project, cancelled in 1959 in the belief that all future aerial defence would be undertaken by ground-launched missiles.

Under a heavy cloud of uncertainty, the British Aircraft Corporation TSR.2 made its maiden flight in September 1964. Having completed just 24 flights, the prototype was grounded and the project cancelled in April 1965. None of the other aircraft near completion on the production line were ever to fly.

The TSR.2 (the initials stood for tactical strike and reconnaissance) was a truly revolutionary design and, had it not been cancelled, would still have been a front-line aircraft more than two decades later. Apart from its remarkable performance, its advanced avionics were far superior to any other systems available at that time. The determination of the UK government to see the end of the project meant that the manufacturers were instructed to destroy all 17 of the development aircraft then on the final production line, together with the production jigs, so that the project could not be revived at a later date.

Three airframes survived. One went ot a gunnery range for target practice, while a second found its way to the Imperial War Museum's collection at Duxford near Cambridge. The third example, which never took to the air, found shelter with the RAF's Historic Aircraft collection.

Above: The TSR.2 at the Imperial War Museum, Duxford, Cambridgeshire.

BRITISH AIRCRAFT CORPORATION TSR.2
COUNTRY OF ORIGIN
UK
ENGINES
two 30,610 lb st (13,885 kg st) Bristol Siddeley Olympus 320 turbojets
CREW
two
MAX SPEED
1,360 mph (2,185 km/h)
RANGE
2,300 miles (3,706 km)
CEILING
60,000 ft (18,290 m)
LENGTH
89 ft 0 in (27.13 m)
SPAN
37 ft 0 in (11.28 m)
HEIGHT
24 ft 0 in (7.32 m)

ROYAL AIR FORCE MUSEUM COLLECTION AEROSPACE MUSEUM	
OWNER/OPERATOR :	Royal Air Force Museum Collection
ADDRESS :	RAF Cosford, Wolverhampton, West Midlands, WV7 3EX
LOCATION :	8 miles northwest of Wolverhampton. Road – off the A41
ADMISSION :	April-October 1000-1600 daily; November-March 1000-1800 Monday-Friday
FURTHER INFO :	As well as being a major part of the Royal Air Force Museum Collection, Cosford is also home to the British Airways collection of airliners used by BA and its predecessors since 1945.

Boeing B-17 Fortress

The United States Army Air Force and the Royal Air Force held different views on the most effective way strategically to attack Germany during World War II. The British had developed night bombing techniques, and therefore designed their bombers to carry less defensive armament than their US counterparts, who had elected for daylight bombing with its greater risk of fighter attack.

As such, the standard USAAF bomber of the war became the Boeing B-17 Fortress, so named because it bristled with machine guns. The later models were fitted with twin 0.5-inch Brownings in chin, dorsal, ball and tail turrets, plus two in nose sockets, another in the radio compartment and one in each waist position.

Boeing first flew their B-17 in July 1935, developed to meet a United States Army Air Corps requirement, using experience gained with their Model 247 transport. While the first variants to see service in Europe were found somewhat lacking, the re-designed B-17E, which featured a new rear section to improve high altitude performance, and subsequent models became the mainstay of the United States Army Eighth Air Force.

To ease production difficulties, most of the 12,731 examples built came from Lockheed and Douglas factories. A somewhat surprisingly large number of B-17s still exist. Many are in flying condition, either as museum pieces or, even now, with commercial operators for uses such as water-bombing forest fires.

The Mud Island leisure complex at Memphis, Tennessee proudly displays B-17F *Memphis Belle*, the best-known US bomber of World War II, and star of the recent Steven Spielberg film of the same name.

Right: The Boeing B-17 Fortress at Mud Island.

Below: At the Confederate Air Force Base in Mesa, Arizona.

MUD ISLAND LEISURE COMPLEX		
OWNER/OPERATOR	:	Memphis City
ADDRESS	:	125 North Front Street, Memphis, Tennessee 38103
LOCATION	:	In the western part of the city
ADMISSION	:	April-October 1000-2200 daily; November, December, March 1000-1700 daily
FURTHER INFO	:	*Memphis Belle* is situated in its own specially constructed pavilion.

BOEING B-17 FORTRESS	
COUNTRY OF ORIGIN	
USA	
ENGINES	
four Wright R-1820-65 Cyclone 9-cylinder radial air-cooled 1,200 hp each	
CREW	
nine	
MAX SPEED	
317 mph (510 km/h) at 25,000 ft (7,620 m)	
RANGE	
3,300 miles (4,800 km)	
CEILING	
36,000 ft (11,150 m)	
LENGTH	
73 ft 10 in (22.50 m)	
SPAN	
103 ft 9 in (31.62 m)	
HEIGHT	
19 ft 2 in (5.84 m)	

BOEING B-29 SUPERFORTRESS

BOEING B-29-45-MO SUPERFORTRESS
COUNTRY OF ORIGIN
USA
ENGINES
four 2,200 hp Wright Cyclone air-cooled radial
CREW
ten
MAX SPEED
358 mph (576 km/h)
RANGE
4,100 miles (6,600 km)
CEILING
31,850 ft (9,700 m)
LENGTH
99 ft 0 in (30.18 m)
SPAN
141 ft 3 in (43.05 m)
HEIGHT
29 ft 7 in (9.02 m)

There is a touch of irony that the aircraft which unleashed the holocaust of the world's first atomic bomb dropped in anger ended up near-derelict at the end of a runway on a USAF base. The irony goes further; just as the Japanese city of Hiroshima was rebuilt following that fateful attack on 6 August 1945, the Boeing B-29 Superfortress *Enola Gay* was rescued from its fate of decay to be restored for permanent display.

Piloted by Col Paul W Tibbets, Jr, *Enola Gay* entered the history books at 8.15 am on 6 August 1945, when the six-ton (6,096 kg) atomic bomb nicknamed 'Little Boy' was released over Hiroshima. Fifty seconds later, the bomb exploded with the force of 20,000 tons (20,400 tonnes) of TNT, destroying 4.7 square miles (7.5 km²) of the city centre, leaving 71,379 dead and over 68,000 injured.

Three days after the Hiroshima attack, a sister ship, *Bock's Car*, captained by Lt Col Charles W Sweeney, dropped the second operational atomic bomb on the city of Nagasaki. The two attacks quickly brought an end to the Second World War with the Japanese officially surrendering on 2 September 1945.

Today, *Enola Gay* is in the care of the world-renowned Smithsonian Institution's National Air and Space Museum. It is presently at the museum's Paul E Garber Facility, where it is being restored to display condition.

The museum is possibly the world's most important aircraft collection. Many of its most famous exhibits, including the Wright Flyer and Lindbergh's *Spirit of St Louis* can be seen at the Smithsonian Institution in Washington DC.

NATIONAL AIR AND SPACE MUSEUM	
OWNER/OPERATOR :	Smithsonian Institution
ADDRESS :	Paul E Garber Facility, Silver Hill Road, Suitland, Maryland
LOCATION :	6 miles (9.6 km) southeast of Washington DC
ADMISSION :	Tours by appointment Monday-Friday 1000; Saturday & Sunday 1000 & 1300
FURTHER INFO :	The Garber Facility is the outstation to the main museum and contains the restoration workshops. Some 140 aircraft are on display.

BOEING B–47 STRATOJET

Following their established tradition of producing highly successful heavy bombers, Boeing approached the task of their first jet-powered derivative as soon as a suitable powerplant was available.

Meanwhile, although originally designed as a piston-engined bomber, the North American B-45 Tornado became the first four-engined jet aircraft to fly in the United States when it took to the air in March 1947. Just 139 were produced, and the last reconnaissance version was finally withdrawn in 1958. In comparison, some 1,800 Boeing B-47 Stratojets were produced from the prototype of 1947 to the final production aircraft of 1957 and remained in service until the mid 1960s.

The first succesful long-range jet bomber, the B-47 also saw service in photo-reconnaissance and weather research roles, in addition to specialist uses as a missile target drone, crew trainer and special trials platform. Powered by six General Electric J47s, the B-47 was manufactured by Douglas at Tulsa and Lockheed at Marietta as well as Boeing at Wichita. With its distinctive cigar-shaped fuselage and narrow highly swept-back wings, it was a familiar sight in the skies over Europe, Japan and northern Canada, as well as the United States.

As headquarters of the Strategic Air Command, it is natural that Offutt Air Force Base features a B-47 within its comprehensive collection of strategic bombers used by SAC.

BOEING B-47E STRATOJET	
COUNTRY OF ORIGIN	
USA	
ENGINES	
six General Electric J47-GE-25 turbojets, 6,000 lb (2,721 kg) thrust each	
CREW	
three	

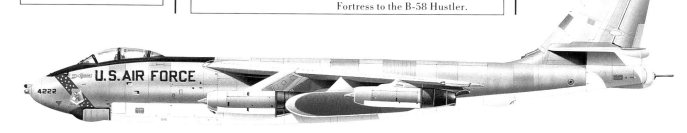

STRATEGIC AIR COMMAND MUSEUM

OWNER/OPERATOR :		United States Air Force
ADDRESS	:	2510 Clay Street, Belleville, Nebraska 68005
LOCATION	:	10 miles south of Omaha. Road – Interstate 80
ADMISSION	:	Daily 0800-1700
FURTHER INFO	:	Among the types exhibited, the bombers represent most types used by SAC from the B-17 Fortress to the B-58 Hustler.

Inset Bottom Left: The B-47E on display at Plattsburgh Military Museum, New York.

MAX SPEED
606 mph (975 km/h) at 16,300 ft (4,968 m)
RANGE
4,000 miles (6,435 km)
CEILING
40,500 ft (12,345 m)
LENGTH
109 ft 10 in (33.4 7 m)
SPAN
116 ft (35.35 m)
HEIGHT
27 ft 11 in (8.50 m)

BRISTOL F. 2B FIGHTER

he development of aircraft design between the start of World War I in 1914, and the appearance of the later types in 1917 and 1918, was truly dramatic. Many superb designs had been introduced by the warring nations, but the appearance of the Bristol Fighter firmly put the balance of air power in the laps of the Allied forces.

Variously described as 'one of the classic aircraft of World War I', and 'a fighter which can be considered one of the very best of the war' among many other accolades, the two-seat Bristol F.2 was designed in March 1916 by Captain Frank S Barnwell who, dissatisfied with existing Allied types, wanted to produce a fighter to match the German types of the time.

The F.2 met with disaster on its first mission when all six aircraft were engaged and shot down by a similar number of Albatross D.IIIs, with the loss of the all 12 airmen. The fault, however, was found to be not with the aircraft, but the fact that the fliers had not been trained in the use of a forward firing weapon which the F.2 carried in addition to the rear gun.

Together with better trained aircrew, the impoved F.2B, with a more powerful engine and greater range, took over the skies during the later phases of the war. It remained in RAF service until as late as 1932, being used for army co-operation duties.

Of the 5,308 machines produced, just four remain, all in the UK. One is still airworthy with the Shuttleworth Collection, who have a policy of maintaining their historic aircraft in flying condition wherever possible.

BRISTOL F.2B FIGHTER	
COUNTRY OF ORIGIN	
UK	
ENGINES	
Rolls-Royce Falcon III 12-cylinder liquid-called inline V, 257 hp	
CREW	
two	
MAX SPEED	
123 mph (198 km/h) at 5,000 ft (1,524 m)	
ENDURANCE	
3 hours	
CEILING	
21,500 ft (6,553 m)	
LENGTH	
25 ft 10 in (7.87 m)	
SPAN	
39 ft 3 in (11.96 m)	
HEIGHT	
9 ft 9 in (2.97 m)	

THE SHUTTLEWORTH COLLECTION		
OWNER/OPERATOR	:	The Shuttleworth Trust
ADDRESS	:	Old Warden Aerodrome, Biggleswade, Bedfordshire SG18 9ER
LOCATION	:	3 miles west of Biggleswade. Road – near A1
ADMISSION	:	Daily 1000-1700 (or dusk if earlier)
FURTHER INFO	:	A superb collection, unique in that it is the only one in Europe with a cross section of original aircraft dating from the first years of aviation to the present day.

DASSAULT MD.450 OURAGAN

The first jet fighter of French design to be ordered in quantity, the Dassault Ouragan first flew on 28 February 1949, powered by a licence-built Rolls-Royce Nene turbojet. 362 examples were ordered by the French Air Force, equipping four fighter wings in 1952. In 1953 the Indian Air Force placed an order for 71 aircraft, and in February 1957 13 more were shipped to India aboard the French aircraft carrier Dixmude. Named *Toofani* (Whirlwind) in Indian service, the Ouragan began to be replaced by the Mystère IV in 1958, but remained in service as an operational trainer until well into the 1960s.

The second overseas customer was the Israeli Air Force, which received an initial batch of Ouragans in November 1955. During the next two years the number of Ouragans supplied to Israel rose to 75. The aircraft saw action in the Arab-Israeli war of 1956 and proved capable of absorbing considerable battle damage, although they were distinctly inferior to the MiG-15s used by the Egyptian Air Force. As in India, the Ouragan was used for some years in the operational training role after being phased out of first-line service. In addition to its built-in armament of four 20 mm cannon, the Ouragan could carry a variety of bombs and rocket projectiles, and during the Arab-Israeli war it took part in some notable ground attack missions, particularly against the Egyptian 1st Armoured Division in Sinai. Rocket-firing Ouragans also disabled the Egyptian destroyer *Ibrahim el Awal*, which was captured by the Israeli Navy.

In 1975 Israel supplied 18 of her surviving Ouragans to El Salvador, which was still using them in the 1980s for ground-attack operations against left-wing guerrilla forces. Five of the Ouragans were destroyed in 1982 during a guerrilla raid on their base at Ilopango.

Main picture: An example of the Ouragon at the Indian Air Force Museum in Palam.

Inset: The Ouragon at the Aeroclub de la Somme.

ABBEVILLE AIRFIELD	
OWNER/OPERATOR :	Aero Club de la Somme
ADDRESS :	Drucat, Abbeville 80, France
LOCATION :	Outside the motel at the airfield
ADMISSION :	Free access
FURTHER INFO :	The well-weathered aircraft has been on display at the airport since at least 1967.

DASSAULT MD.450 OURAGAN	
COUNTRY OF ORIGIN	France
ENGINES	Hispano-Suiza Nene 104B turbojet, 5,000 lb (2,270 kg) thrust
CREW	one
MAX SPEED	584 mph (940 km/h) at sea level
RANGE	570 miles (920 km)
CEILING	43,000 ft (13,000 m)
LENGTH	35 ft 3 in (10.74 m)
SPAN	43 ft 2 in (13.16 m)
HEIGHT	13 ft 7 in (4.14 m)

DE HAVILLAND D.H. 98 MOSQUITO

An all-wooden unarmed bomber, powered by two Rolls-Royce Merlin engines would have appeared to have stood little chance of success in 1939. Merlin engines were in short supply and badly needed to power Spitfire and Hurricane fighters.

Geoffrey de Havilland, however, had confidence in his company's design, owing to the success of the Comet racer and the Albatross airliner, and he developed the project as a private venture, even though the Air Ministry showed little interest. Less than 11 months elapsed between the eventual Ministry go-ahead and the first flight of the Mosquito prototype on 25 November 1940. The performance surprised even de Havilland's engineers and the Mosquito remained the world's fastest operational aircraft until the introduction of jet aircraft some two and a half years later.

Built in the UK, Australia and Canada, 7,718 aircraft were produced in 40 different marks. As well as the original bomber design, Mosquitos were also produced as night fighters, fighter bombers, photo reconnaissance and trainers while some were converted for target towing duties. The original prototype, designed and built at Salisbury Hall, a 17th-century house near de Havilland's factory, was flown in a distinctive all-yellow colour scheme so that British anti-aircraft gunners would recognize the unfamiliar shape.

It not only survived the war but also the type's final withdrawal from RAF service in 1963. Meanwhile, in 1959, the owner of Salisbury Hall had acquired the aircraft and, with the help of enthusiasts, has since built up an impressive museum of de Havilland aircraft and engines and memorabilia.

THE MOSQUITO AIRCRAFT MUSEUM		
ADDRESS	:	Salisbury Hall, London Colney, St Albans, Hertfordshire AL2 1BU
LOCATION	:	5 miles south of St Albans. Road – off M25 Junction 22
ADMISSION	:	Easter-September 1400-1800 (Sundays) 1030-1230, 1400-1730 (Bank Holidays)
FURTHER INFO	:	Britain's oldest aircraft museum is in the grounds of the seventeenth-century Salisbury Hall and is dedicated to preserving both aircraft and engines of de Havilland.

Main picture: At the Mosquito Aircraft Museum.
Inset: The Mosquito at Hamilton Airforce Base, Ontario.

DE HAVILLAND MOSQUITO
COUNTRY OF ORIGIN
UK
ENGINES
two Rolls-Royce Merlin XXI 12-cylinder V liquid-cooled, 1,460 hp each
CREW
two
MAX SPEED
380 mph (611 km/h) at 17,000 ft (5,200 m)
RANGE
2,180 miles (3,500 km)
CEILING
35,000 ft (10,600 m)
LENGTH
40 ft 6 in (12.34 m)
SPAN
54 ft 2 in (16.51 m)
HEIGHT
12 ft 6 in (3.81 m)

DE HAVILLAND D.H. 100 VAMPIRE

Air observers had no trouble in recognizing the de Havilland Vampire, no matter how bad the weather, because of the distinctive whistling sound as it flew overhead. Any doubters should visit an airshow when the RAF 'Vintage Pair' display team, consisting of a Vampire and a Gloster Meteor, are performing.

Britain's second operational jet fighter, the Vampire made its first flight on 20 September 1943, although it did not enter service until May 1946. The prototype was given the unlikely name of 'Spider Crab' before the Vampire was adopted.

Although the Vampire was too late to see war service, it was a huge success, and over 4,000 were built and supplied to some 30 air forces around the world. The production total included numerous examples built under licence in Australia, France, India and Italy.

The original F.1 model was followed by many other variants culminating in the DH.115 Vampire T.11 side-by-side seat advanced trainer which equipped the RAF's flying schools until late 1967. Over 800 were built, as well as some 200 more under licence. On disposal, many RAF T.11s were allocated to Air Training Corps units but problems in maintaining the airframes meant that many wasted away.

The mark FB.52 was an export version of the FB.5 fighter bomber supplied to South Africa and many other countries. Numerous examples of the Vampire remain in South Africa including a FB.52 at the National Museum in Bloemfontein.

Above: The Vampire at the Royal Air Force Museum in Wales.

RAF ST. ATHAN HISTORIC AIRCRAFT COLLECTION	
OWNER/OPERATOR :	Royal Air Force Museum
ADDRESS :	RAF St. Athan, Barry, South Glamorgan, Wales
LOCATION :	About 12 miles (20 km) west of Cardiff. Road – B4265 to Cowbridge
ADMISSION :	First Sunday in every month 1400-1700 otherwise prior permission only
FURTHER INFO :	This outpost of the Royal Air Force Museum is due for closure, the aircraft eventually being moved to the museum's other collections.

DE HAVILLAND D.H.100 VAMPIRE	
COUNTRY OF ORIGIN	
UK	
ENGINES	
de Havilland Goblin 2 turbojet, 3,100 lb (1,420 kg) thrust	
CREW	
one	
MAX SPEED	
548 mph (882 km/h) at 30,000 ft (9,145 m)	

RANGE	
1,220 miles (1,960 km)	
CEILING	
44,000 ft (13,410 m)	
LENGTH	
30 ft 9 in (9.37 m)	
SPAN	
38 ft 0 in (11.58 m)	
HEIGHT	
8 ft 10 in (2.69 m)	

ENGLISH ELECTRIC LIGHTNING

The first and only purely British-designed and built supersonic fighter for the Royal Air Force was the distinctive English Electric (later British Aircraft Corporation) Lightning. Unique in its configuration, the design originated in the P.1A and P.1B experimental aircraft which thrilled the crowds in the late 1950s at the Farnborough Air Show – the shop window of Britain's aircraft industry.

The first P.1A prototype made its maiden flight in the hands of test pilot Roland Beamont on 4 August 1954, with the second taking to the air on 18 July 1955. Two P.1Bs and three Lightning prototypes followed, together with 20 pre-production machines before series production began.

The Lightning entered service with the Royal Air Force in 1960, with No 74 (Tiger) Squadron. Part of their duties was to act as the official RAF air display team, superseding the famous Black Arrows, 111 Squadron with their Hawker Hunter aircraft.

Following withdrawal from service in 1988, the Ministry of Defence put their remaining Lightnings up for sale at knock-down prices. As a result, many examples have ended their days in aircraft collections, with at least one group attempting to put a T.4 trainer variant back into flying condition.

The second prototype P.1A, WG763, survives as an exhibit at the Museum of Science and Industry in Manchester, which contains an excellent Aviation Gallery. The location is fitting since the P.1 and the subsequent Lightning were designed and built in English Electric's factories in the same region.

MUSEUM OF SCIENCE AND INDUSTRY AVIATION GALLERY

OWNER/OPERATOR	:	Museum of Science and Industry
ADDRESS	:	Liverpool Road, Castlefield, Manchester M3 4JP
LOCATION	:	Manchester City Centre
ADMISSION	:	Every day 1030-1700
FURTHER INFO	:	The museum has been created around the world's first passenger railway station.

Top right: The P.1A, the prototype for the Lightning, at the Museum of Science and Industry in Manchester.
Inset: The Lightning T-4.
Below: The Lightning F.1A, at Leuchars Air Force Base in Scotland.

ENGLISH ELECTRIC P.1A

COUNTRY OF ORIGIN	**RANGE**
UK	n/a
ENGINES	**CEILING**
two 10,200 lb s t (4,630 kg s t) Bristol Siddeley Sapphire turbojets	50,000 ft 0 in (15,500 m)
	LENGTH
CREW	50 ft 0 in (15.5 m)
one	**SPAN**
	34 ft 10 in (10.82 m)
MAX SPEED	**HEIGHT**
1,520 mph (2,447 km/h) or Mach 2.3 at altitude	19 ft 7 in (6.06 m)

FAIREY FIREFLY

The Fairey Firefly was a wartime design which entered service with the Fleet Air Arm in 1943. It saw much operational service before the end of hostilities, including attacks on the German battleship *Tirpitz*, a strike on the Japanese-held oil refineries in Sumatra and missions over the Japanese home islands while operating with Task Force 57 in the Pacific. The Firefly also equipped eight FAA squadrons at the end of World War II. Most of these were subsequently disbanded, but from October 1945, 11 other FAA units re-equipped with the type. These were mostly the Firefly FR.4 or FR.5, but one – 827 Squadron – was still using the earlier FR.1 in 1949, and in December that year it began a series of strikes against terrorist hideouts in Malaya, flying from the light fleet carrier HMS *Triumph*. 827 Squadron was also the first Firefly squadron to see action in Korea, on 30 June 1950. The Firefly continued to operate with considerable success throughout the Korean War, serving with 810 Squadron (HMS *Theseus*), 812 and 820 (HMS *Glory*), 817 (HMAS *Sydney*) and 825 (HMS *Ocean*).

The Firefly AS.6 was a three-seat anti-submarine variant which entered service in 1951 and equipped five Fleet Air Arm squadrons, as well as six squadrons of the Royal Naval Volunteer Reserve. In 1954, the Firefly AS.6s of 825 Squadron carried out a series of ground attack missions against terrorists in Malaya, the last occasion the type fired its guns in anger.

Total production of the Firefly (all marks, up to the U Mk 8 target drone) was 1,702 aircraft, and the type was supplied to Australia, Canada, Denmark, Ethiopia, India, the Netherlands, Sweden and Thailand. The Dutch aircraft – FR.1s – saw action against rebel forces in the Dutch East Indies.

WAR MEMORIAL		
ADDRESS	:	Griffith, New South Wales, Australia
LOCATION	:	In the town centre
ADMISSION	:	Free access
FURTHER INFO	:	The Royal Australian Navy operated the Fairey Firefly from August 1948–March 1966.

FAIREY FIREFLY		RANGE
COUNTRY OF ORIGIN		1,300 miles (2,100 km)
UK		**CEILING**
ENGINES		28,000 ft (8,500 m)
Rolls-Royce Griffon 11B 12-cylinder V liquid-cooled, 1,730 hp		**LENGTH**
		37 ft 7 in (11.46 m)
CREW		**SPAN**
two		44 ft 6 in (13.56 m)
MAX SPEED		**HEIGHT**
316 mph (508 km/h) at 14,000 ft (4,250 m)		13 ft 7 in (4.14 m)

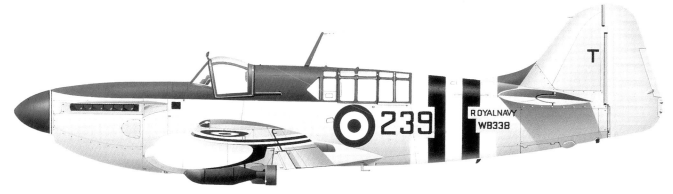

FMA IA–58 PUCARA

A°n indigenous design built by Argentina's Fabrica Militar de Aviones (FMA), the Pucara was produced in response for a light attack aircraft for the air force.

For use in both the counter-insurgency and close-support roles, design started in 1966 and the first prototype made its first flight on 20 August, 1969. Production did not commence until 1974 and the initial orders for 45 aircraft began reaching operational units in 1976.

A sleek twin-turboprop powered aircraft with a good all-round performance, the Pucara was, however, an unsophisticated design. Heavily used in the Falklands conflict of 1982, some 24 were lost to British attacks. To improve the aircraft's capabilities, a revised version known as the IA-58C Pucara Charlie was flown in 1985. A single-seater, it featured improved avionics and equipment and carried a greater range of armaments.

Following the conflict, several examples were taken to the UK for evaluation and museum display. One example remained at RAF Stanley airfield where, under the direction of Mark

FALKLAND ISLANDS MUSEUM	
ADDRESS	: Port Stanley, Falkland Islands
LOCATION	: One for display at Port Stanley
ADMISSION	: Not available
FURTHER INFO	: The Pucara and a Bell UH-1H Huey are being stored at RAF Mount Pleasant awaiting completion of the museum.

Harrisson, it was rebuilt by volunteers from both the Army and RAF.

Registered A-529, the Pucara received parts from sister ships A-514 and A-509 while other items, such as the propellers and canopy perspex were made locally. During the restoration work, the aircraft was completely stripped down, protected and rebuilt.

Above and right: The Falkland Island Museum, and the Aerospace Museum in Shropshire both exhibit examples of the Pucara.

FMA IA-58 PUCARA	
COUNTRY OF ORIGIN	**RANGE**
Argentina	1,890 miles (3,042 km)
ENGINES	**CEILING**
two Turbomeca Astazou XVIG turboprops, 1,022 hp each	32,810 ft (10,000 m)
CREW	**LENGTH**
two	46 ft 9 in (14.25 m)
MAX SPEED	**SPAN**
	47 ft 7 in (14.50 m)
310 mph (500 km/h)	**HEIGHT**
	17 ft 7 in (5.36 m)

FOCKE–WULF FW 190

riginally designed as a result of a German air ministry suggestion that Focke-Wulfe should develop a fighter to be built concurrently with the Messerschmitt Bf 109, the Fw 190 became Germany's best fighter of World War II.

Designer Kurt Tank produced two proposals and, despite some misgivings, the version chosen was powered by an air-cooled radial engine. Three prototypes were constructed, the first flying on 1 June 1939. Despite early problems with overheating, initial trials went very well for Germany's first radial-engined monoplane fighter.

The Fw 190 went into service during July 1941 and immediately proved itself to be faster and more manoeuvrable than the Spitfire V. Numerous developments followed as 13,367 machines were produced in ten versions as interceptors while a further 6,634 were built in two versions as fighter-bombers.

The ultimate fighter version was the Fw 190D which was powered by a Junkers Jumo liquid-cooled inline engine which, with power boost, gave a maximum speed of 453 mph (729 km/h) at 37,000 ft (11,470 m). With the increased performance the D model was a match for the North American P-51D Mustang.

Five Fw 190Ds were brought to the United States for evaluation after the war and one survived with the Georgia Technical University. Having been purchased by Doug Champlin for his Fighter Museum in Mesa, Arizona in 1972, the aircraft was returned to Germany for restoration by Arthur Williams, helped by no other than Kurt Tank himself.

The aircraft returned to the United States in 1976, where it takes pride of place in the Champlin Fighter Museum.

CHAMPLIN FIGHTER MUSEUM

OWNER/OPERATOR	:	Doug Champlin
ADDRESS	:	4636 Fighter Aces Drive, Mesa, Arizona 85205
LOCATION	:	Falcon Field Airport, 3 miles north of Mesa
ADMISSION	:	Daily 1000-1700 (except public holidays)
FURTHER INFO	:	The museum is the home of the American Fighter Aces Association who have a large collection of memorabilia on display.

FOCKE-WULF Fw 190A-1

COUNTRY OF ORIGIN
Germany
ENGINES
BMW 801C-1 14-cylinder radial air-cooled, 1,600 hp
CREW
one
MAX SPEED
389 mph (626 km/h)
RANGE
497 miles (800 km)
CEILING
34,775 ft (10,600 m)
LENGTH
29 ft 0 in (8.84 m)
SPAN
34 ft 5½ in (10.50 m)
HEIGHT
12 ft 11½ in (3.94 m)

Top: The Focke Wulf in the collection of Doug Champlin.

Above: The model at the National Air and Space Museum, Silver Hill, Maryland.

GLOSTER METEOR

Arguably the most successful of the first generation jet fighters, the Gloster Meteor was the only Allied jet aircraft to see service during World War II.

The initial order for eight prototypes and 20 production F.1s was placed in September 1941. While the first prototype was completed in mid-1942 and taxying trials took place immediately, the first flight of the type did not occur until 5 March 1943 because of a lack of engines that could produce sufficient power.

The first squadron to fly the Meteor operationally during the war was No 616, who received their first aircraft on 12 July 1944. The aircraft was to stay in front-line service with the Royal Air Force in various marks until July 1961, by which time 3,850 had been built in the UK and the Netherlands under licence and supplied to some 12 air forces worldwide.

Following the end of hostilities, several Meteor F.4s were transferred to the RAF's High Speed Flight. In modified form, they were used to raise the world air speed record to 606 mph (976 km/h) on 7 November 1945, and then 616 mph (992 km/h) the following 7 September, the aircraft being flown by Gp Capt E M Donaldson.

Initially named the Rampage or Thunderbolt (the latter name was dropped because of confusion with the Republic design of the same name), the Meteor nearly gathered yet another name tag. Designed and funded as a private venture, the Gloster G44 ground attack development of the Meteor incorporated a strengthened F.4 wing and F.8 rear fuselage. Named the Reaper, it first flew in 1951, but with the company lacking any orders, the sole example was de-militarized in 1954 and converted to a T.7, ending its days with Svedino's Bil Och Flygmuseum in Sweden.

SVEDINO'S BIL OCH FLYGMUSEUM	
OWNER/OPERATOR :	Lennart Svedfelt
ADDRESS :	Vgglarp, Sloinge 531050, Sweden
LOCATION :	Approx. 25 km northwest of Halmstad on the coast road to Falkenberg
ADMISSION :	April-October (except July, August) Saturday-Sunday 1000-1700. July-August daily 1000-1700
FURTHER INFO :	Many ex-Swedish air force types share this privately run museum with a number of civil light aircraft and over 120 cars.

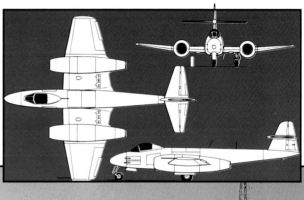

GLOSTER METEOR F.8	RANGE
COUNTRY OF ORIGIN	980 miles (1,580 km)
UK	**CEILING**
ENGINES	43,000 ft (13,106 m)
two Rolls-Royce Derwent 8 turbojets, 3,500 lb (1,587 kg) thrust each	**LENGTH**
	44 ft 7 in (13.58 m)
CREW	**SPAN**
one	37 ft 2 in (11.32 m)
MAX SPEED	**HEIGHT**
598 mph (962 km/h) at 33,000 ft (10,000 m)	13 ft 0 in (3.96 m)

Main picture: The Gloster Meteor F8 at RAF Woodvale.
Inset: The Reaper at the Flygmuseum in Sweden.

GRUMMAN TBF AVENGER

The Grumman TBF Avenger torpedo-bomber was designed to replace the Douglas Devastator, which suffered heavy losses during anti-shipping attacks in the early stages of the Pacific War. Two XTBF-1 prototypes were ordered by the US Navy in April 1940, and a substantial production order had been placed by the time the first of these flew on 1 August 1941. The first production TBF-1s went into service with Squadron VT-8 in January 1942. Its combat debut was inauspicious — five out of six aircraft were shot down by Japanese Zero fighters during an heroic but unsuccessful attack by VT-8 on enemy warships during the Battle of Midway — but it went on to become one of the most celebrated naval attack aircraft ever, widely used in the Atlantic as well as the Pacific.

Up to December 1943 Grumman built 2,293 Avengers, of which 402 were supplied to the Royal Navy and 63 to the Royal New Zealand Air Force. Avenger production was also undertaken by the Eastern Aircraft Division of General Motors, which built 2,882 as the TBM-1 and TBM-1C. Of these, 334 went to the Royal Navy as Avenger IIs. Eastern went on to complete 4,665 TBM-3s, with wings strengthened to carry rocket projectiles or a radar pod; 222 of these became the Royal Navy's Avenger III. Because of some difficulty in installing British torpedos in the American aircraft, the RN Avengers were used as bombers, minelayers or rocket-firing strike aircraft. Until January 1944, when the name Avenger was standardized, the British aircraft were known as Tarpons.

American and British Avengers played an important role in the final assault on Japan, and the type remained in service for many years after the war.

MUSEUM OF TRANSPORT & TECHNOLOGY		
ADDRESS	:	Great North Road, Western Springs, Auckland 2, New Zealand
LOCATION	:	2 miles southwest of the city centre
ADMISSION	:	Daily 0900-1700
FURTHER INFO	:	The museum represents all types of transport and holds regular 'live' weekends. The main site is connected by a tramway to a 20-acre park where the larger aircraft are exhibited.

Below: The Museum of Transport and Technology, Auckland, includes the Avenger in its collection.

GRUMMAN TBF-1 AVENGER	
COUNTRY OF ORIGIN	USA
ENGINES	Wright R-2600-8 Cyclone 14-cylinder radial air-cooled, 1,700 hp
CREW	three
MAX SPEED	271 mph (436 km/h) at 12,000 ft (3,660 m)
RANGE	1,215 miles (1,950 km)
CEILING	22,400 ft (6,800 m)
LENGTH	40 ft 0 in (12.19 m)
SPAN	54 ft 2 in (16.51 m)
HEIGHT	16 ft 5 in (5 m)

Above: The example on display at the Canadian Warplane Heritage, Ontario.

GRUMMAN S2 TRACKER

One of the most important carrier-borne anti-submarine aircraft of the post-war years, the prototype Grumman XS2F-1 Tracker flew for the first time on 4 December 1952. First deliveries were made to Navy Squadron VS-26 in February 1954, and at the end of that year the type embarked on the USS *Princeton* with VS-23. A total of 755 examples of the initial production series of S2F-1s were built, and the type was also supplied to Argentina, Japan, Italy, Brazil, Taiwan, Thailand, Uruguay and the Netherlands.

The S-2C, which was next on the assembly line, featured a larger torpedo bay capable of housing homing torpedoes. Sixty were built, and most of these were later converted to US-2C cargo aircraft. The S-2D was a developed version with an increased wingspan and improved crew accommodation, as well as more advanced weaponry and avionics. It had twice the endurance of the S2F-1 (or S-2A, as it was later redesignated) when giving 'round the fleet' anti-submarine coverage at a radius of 230 miles. The S-2E was an upgraded version with still more advanced equipment, and could carry 5-inch rockets on underwing racks.

The S-2A Tracker was built under licence in Canada by de Havilland Aircraft Ltd, the Canadian version being designated CS2F-1. Further variants were the CS2F-2 and CS2F-3. The first two versions were operated from shore bases, while the CS2F-3 was used by Squadron VS-880 aboard the carrier HMCS *Bonaventure*. Of the 100 CS2F-1 Trackers built in Canada, 17 were supplied to the Royal Netherlands Navy and 12 to the Brazilian Navy, the latter batch operating from the carrier *Minas Gerais*. Variants of the basic Tracker design were the C-1A Trader general purpose aircraft and the E-1B Tracer, which was modified for early warning and fighter direction.

INTREPID AIR-SEA-SPACE MUSEUM		
OWNER/OPERATOR	:	Intrepid Foundation
ADDRESS	:	Intrepid Square, West 46th Street and 12th Avenue, New York 10036
LOCATION	:	Pier 86 on the west side of Manhattan Island
ADMISSION	:	Wednesday-Sunday 1000-1700
FURTHER INFO	:	The aircraft are aboard *USS Intrepid*, an aircraft carrier launched in 1943 and served with distinction before becoming a floating city-centre museum in 1980.

Top: The Grumman S2-E Tracker at the Intrepid Air-Sea-Space Museum, New York.

Bottom: The Grumman C-1 Trader, photographed at Pensacola, Florida.

GRUMMAN S-2A TRACKER
COUNTRY OF ORIGIN
USA
ENGINES
two Wright R-1820-82 WA Cyclone 9-cylinder air-cooled radials, 1,525 hp each
CREW
four
MAX SPEED
287 mph (461 km/h) at 5,000 ft (1,524 m)
RANGE
900 miles (1,450 km)
CEILING
23,000 ft (7,010 m)
LENGTH
42 ft 3 in (12.87 m)
SPAN
69 ft 8 in (21.23 m)
HEIGHT
16 ft 3 in (4.95 m)

HAWKER HURRICANE

lthough the Spitfire took the glory for the RAF's success during the Battle of Britain, the brunt of the fighting was borne by the Hawker Hurricane. Less agile and with a lower performance, the Hurricane was nevertheless a very rugged aircraft which could absorb a lot of punishment.

The Hurricane began as a private venture, with the RAF placing its first orders in June 1936, seven months after its first flight. It was not only the first monoplane fighter in RAF service, but it outnumbered the Spitfire by two to one in the Battle of Britain. It saw service as a light bomber in the Western Desert, a night fighter in the Far East and a convoy protector at sea. It was catapulted off merchant ships (the pilot having to make for a shore base, or ditch near the convoy and be picked up) and served as the Sea Hurricane (the 'Hurricat') on aircraft carriers.

Hurricanes served with air forces around the world, and were produced in Canada in large numbers fitted with American-built Merlin engines. They also saw service in Russia in the form of modified two-seat ground attack aircraft with tandem cockpits.

Although over 14,000 Hurricanes were built (the last, a Mark IV, flew in 1944), the type soon disappeared from RAF service

INDIAN AIR FORCE MUSEUM	
OWNER/OPERATOR :	Indian Air Force
ADDRESS :	Palam Airport, New Delhi, India
LOCATION :	9 miles southwest of Delhi
ADMISSION :	Daily (excluding Tuesday) 1000-1330
FURTHER INFO :	The aircraft collection is in a hangar on the air force base. A collection of items (uniforms, equipment, documents, etc) depicting the history of the IAF is displayed in a barracks nearby.

after the end of World War II. Compared with the Spitfire, which saw service until the late 1950s, very few examples remain today.

Delivered to the Indian Air Force as a Mark IIB, Hurricane AP832 is one that did survive and can be seen in the Air Force Museum at Palam, near New Delhi.

Above: One of the few flying examples, this Hurricane belongs to the Canadian Warplane Heritage, Ontario.

Left: The Hurricane at the Indian Air Force Museum.

HAWKER HURRICANE MK1	RANGE
	460 miles (740 km)
COUNTRY OF ORIGIN	**CEILING**
UK	33,200 ft (10,120 m)
ENGINES	**LENGTH**
Rolls-Royce Merlin II 12-cylinder V air-cooled	31 ft 5 in (9.55 m)
CREW	**SPAN**
one	40 ft 0 in (12.19 m)
MAX SPEED	**HEIGHT**
320 mph (515 km/h) at 20,000 ft (6,100 m)	13 ft 1 in (3.99 m)

HAWKER HUNTER

One of the most successful jet fighters ever built, the Hawker Hunter was designed by Sir Sydney Camm, whose work spanned a 40-year period from the Hart biplane fighter of the 1930s, to the VTOL Harrier, and included the Hurricane. The Hunter's clean lines belie the fact that it was a potent fighter aircraft, which in later models was just as useful in the ground attack role. Designed as a replacement for the Gloster Meteor, the prototype made its first flight on 20 July 1951.

As a measure of success, Hunter production ran to nearly 2,000 with over 400 machines being supplied to some 20 countries and 445 built under licence in the Netherlands. Furthermore, more than 700 ex-RAF Hunters were rebuilt for export, mainly to third-world countries.

The prototype, WB188, was modified to F.3 standard and fitted with a Rolls-Royce Avon RA7R. Flown in this form by chief test pilot Neville Duke, it took the air speed record for the UK at a speed of 727.6 mph (1,171.4 km/h).

While WB188 has been preserved in non-flying condition by the RAF Museum, other examples have been purchased by civilians and returned to a flyable state. One such example is operated by Hunter One Collection, and can be seen at air shows throughout Europe, while at least four machines have crossed the Atlantic and are now flying in the United States.

Authentically painted in the colours of No 54 Squadron, RAF, N611JR is operated by Combat Jets Flying Museum of Houston, Texas.

HAWKER HUNTER F.6	
COUNTRY OF ORIGIN	
UK	
ENGINES	
Rolls-Royce Avon 203 turbojet, 10,000 lb (4,536 kg) thrust	
CREW	
one	
MAX SPEED	
710 mph (1,142 km/h)	

RANGE	
1,900 miles (3,085 km)	
CEILING	
51,500 ft (15,700 m)	
LENGTH	
45 ft 10 in (13.98 m)	
SPAN	
33 ft 8 in (10.26 m)	
HEIGHT	
13 ft 2 in (4.01 m)	

COMBAT JETS FLYING MUSEUM	
OWNER/OPERATOR :	Jim Robinson
ADDRESS :	8802 Travellair, Houston, Texas 77061
LOCATION :	William P Hobby Airport, 7 miles southeast of Houston. Road – Route 35
ADMISSION :	Prior permission only
FURTHER INFO :	This private collection of Jet Warbirds also includes an ex-Polish Air Force MiG-15

Main picture: The Hunter at the Combat Jets Flying Museum, painted in the colours of No 54 Squadron RAF.

Inset: At the Aerospace Museum, Shropshire.

HAWKER SEA FURY

he Sea Fury and its land-based equivalent, the Fury, were designed to meet a British requirement for a long-range fighter suitable for use in the Pacific Theatre of operations. The Fury was cancelled with the end of the war, but the Sea Fury, which had first flown on 21 February 1945, was ordered into production for the Royal Navy, the Admiralty being anxious to fill the gap in performance between the piston-engined Seafire 47 and the introduction of jet aircraft. The first Fleet Air Arm squadron to receive the Sea Fury was No 807, in July 1947, followed by 778, 802, 803 and 805 Squadrons.

In 1948 it was decided to modify the Sea Fury to carry bombs and rockets for the fighter-bomber role with the designation

MUSEO DE PLAYA GIRON		
ADDRESS	:	Playa Giron, Cuba
LOCATION	:	In the town centre
ADMISSION	:	Tuesday-Saturday 1300-1930. Sunday 0930-1300
FURTHER INFO	:	The museum was established to commemorate the Bay of Pigs affair of 1961.

Sea Fury FB.11. Three more Sea Fury squadrons, 801, 804 and 808, had now equipped with the type, and together with 802, 805 and 807 these saw service in the Korean War with the 1st, 17th and 21st Carrier Air Groups aboard the light fleet carriers HMS *Ocean,* HMS *Theseus,* HMS *Glory* and HMAS *Sydney.* The Sea Furies proved extremely effective in the ground attack role, and their pilots also claimed the destruction of two MiG-15 jet fighters.

Sea Furies also served with the Royal Canadian Navy, the Royal Netherlands Navy, the Royal Australian Navy, Pakistan, Burma, Egypt and Cuba. The Burmese aircraft remained operational on counter-insurgency work until the late 1960s, while the Cuban Sea Furies were used to strafe Cuban exiles attempting the abortive 'Bay of Pigs' landing in April 1961.

HAWKER SEA FURY FB.11	
COUNTRY OF ORIGIN	
UK	
ENGINES	
Bristol Centaurus 18 18-cylinder air-cooled radial, 2,480 hp	
CREW	
one	
MAX SPEED	
460 mph (740 km/h) at 18,000 ft (5,485 m)	

RANGE	700 miles (1,130 km)
CEILING	36,000 ft (10,970 m)
LENGTH	34 ft 8 in (10.56 m)
SPAN	38 ft 5 in (11.71 m)
HEIGHT	15 ft 10 in (4.82 m)

HAWKER P.1127 KESTREL

O n 21 October 1960, Bill Bedford, the chief test pilot of Hawker Aircraft, entered the history books by making the first test flight of the revolutionary P.1127 VTOL (Vertical Take-Off and Landing) aircraft. Three decades later, the Harrier, as the P.1127 became in its developed form, remains the only successful fixed wing VTOL jet combat aircraft in service.

Following the initial flight, five more prototypes were constructed and rigorously tested until the emergence of an improved model, the Kestrel. Nine aircraft were completed and evaluated by an experimental Tripartite Squadron consisting of American, British and German pilots.

After six years of development, the first Harrier flew on 31 August 1966 and, after further testing, entered service with the RAF on 1 April 1969. The same year, the United States finally confirmed their interest, and the Harrier was ordered for the Marine Corps. This was followed by orders from Spain and India for use on their aircraft carriers. Further development resulted in the Sea Harrier for the Royal Navy, first flying on 20 August 1978. The type proved its capability during the Falklands conflict, when 28 Sea Harriers using Sidewinder missiles downed 24 aircraft for no combat loss of their own.

Working with McDonnell Douglas, British Aerospace (who had absorbed Hawker) produced a much-modified Harrier called the Harrier II. Utilizing the same basic engine as the earlier model, the new aircraft was given a new high-lift wing, redesigned jet nozzles and other modifications which resulted in a greatly enhanced performance.

Following the end of the Tripartite trials, six Kestrels were sent to the USA where they were designated XV-6A and continued proving flights. Four remain, including NASA520 at the Aerospace Park, Hampton, Virginia.

AEROSPACE PARK AND INFORMATION CENTRE	
OWNER/OPERATOR :	United States Air Force
ADDRESS :	413 West Mercury Boulevard, Hampton, Virginia 23666
LOCATION :	To the north of the city. Road – Route 167
ADMISSION :	Aircraft: permanent view Information centre: daily 0900-1700
FURTHER INFO :	The aircraft and missiles are sited in a 15-acre park adjacent to the information centre.

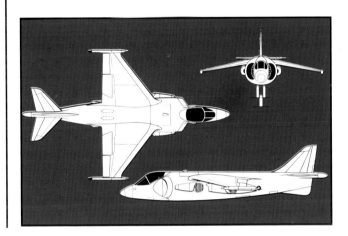

HAWKER P.1127 KESTREL
COUNTRY OF ORIGIN
UK
ENGINES
one Bristol Siddeley Pegasus 5 vectored-thrust turbofan rated at 18,000 lb s t
CREW
one
MAX SPEED
725 mph (1,160 km/h) at 36,000 ft (10,975 m)
RANGE
350 miles (565 km)
CEILING
60,000 ft (18,292 m)
LENGTH
42 ft 6 in (13.70 m)
SPAN
22 ft 11 in (6.97 m)
HEIGHT
10 ft 3 in (3.11 m)

ILYUSHIN IL–28

Designed as a tactical light bomber to replace the piston-engined Tupolev Tu-2, Ilyushin's Il-28 formed the mainstay of the Soviet Bloc's tactical air striking forces during the 1950s and was widely exported to other countries within the Soviet sphere of influence. The aircraft was powered by two Klimov VK-1 turbojets, Russian copies of the Rolls-Royce Nene. The first VK-1-powered Il-28 flew on 20 September 1948 and deliveries to units of the Soviet Frontal Aviation began in the following year, the aircraft's simple and robust construction facilitating mass production. Some examples of the Il-28 appeared on Manchurian bases during the Korean War, but these never ventured over the Yalu River and may have been Soviet Air Force machines.

By 1955 some 800 Il-28s were serving with Eastern Bloc air forces. Early recipients were Poland, Czechoslovakia and China, followed by Romania and Hungary. In 1955-56, 60 were delivered to Egypt, about 20 being destroyed at Luxor in an attack by French Air Force F-84F Thunderstreaks during the Suez crisis. Forty more were delivered in 1957. Most of these deliveries involved ex-Czech aircraft, and in 1958 Indonesia received 35 aircraft from a similar source. Some Egyptian Il-28s, flown by Egyptian crews, operated with the Federal Nigerian Air Force during the Biafra War in 1969.

Other countries using the Il-28 were Algeria, Afghanistan, North Vietnam, North Korea and Cuba. The latter's Il-28 deliveries were a leading factor in the crisis of October 1982, which brought the world to the brink of war, and in fact several shipments were turned back by the US naval blockade.

MUSEUM OREZA POLSKIEGO	
ADDRESS	: Kolobrzeg, Pomerania, Poland
LOCATION	: In the town centre
ADMISSION	: Monday-Wednesday 0930-1300; Thursday-Saturday 0900-1300; Sunday 0830-1230

The Ilyushin IL-28 *below*, was designed to replace the Tupolev Tu-2, *above*.

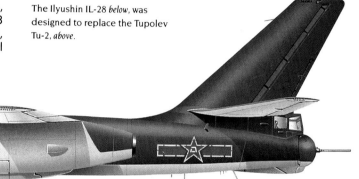

ILYUSHIN IL-28
COUNTRY OF ORIGIN
USSR
ENGINES
two Klimov VK-1 turbojets 6,040 lb (2,740 kg) thrust each
CREW
three
MAX SPEED
559 mph (900 km/h) at 15,000 ft (4,500 m)
RANGE
715 miles (1,135 km)
CEILING
40,355 ft (12,300 m)
LENGTH
57 ft 11 in (17.65 m)
SPAN
70 ft 4 in (21.45 m)
HEIGHT
22 ft 0 in (6.70 m)

JUNKERS JU 87 STUKA

Of the 5,000 Junkers Ju 87 Stuka dive bombers built during their reign of terror as they swept across Europe in support of advancing German ground troops during the early stages of World War II, it is incongruous that just two examples remain in existence today.

With little or no aerial resistance over Europe, the Stuka — an abbreviation of the word *Sturzkampfflugzeug,* which simply means 'dive bomber' — was more a psychological weapon than one of physical destruction.

With such a reputation, the German air crews expected the same result when they turned their attention to the south coast of England at the start of what was to become the Battle of Britain. The Hurricanes and Spitfires of the Royal Air Force soon exposed the vulnerability of the dive-bombing concept and the Ju 87 was quickly transferred to ground-attack duties. Notwithstanding its defeat, the Ju 87 was operational long after it had become obsolete and remained in service until as late as the end of 1944.

Although not a particularly successful aircraft — and perhaps one of the ugliest ever built — the Stuka is possibly the best remembered German aircraft of the war after the Messerschmitt Bf 109.

Of the two remaining examples, one is at the Royal Air Force Museum's Battle of Britain Collection at Hendon, near London. The other is at the unlikely venue of the Museum of Science and Industry in Chicago, Illinois, where it is displayed in the company of an early Supermarine Spitfire Mk.1A credited with five kills in 1940/41.

Below : The interior of the Museum of Science and Industry in Chicago.
Bottom: An example of the Ju 87 at the Battle of Britain Museum.

MUSEUM OF SCIENCE AND INDUSTRY

OWNER/OPERATOR :		Chicago City
ADDRESS	:	57th Street and Lake Shore Drive, Chicago, Illinois 60637
LOCATION	:	4 miles south of the city on the shores of Lake Michigan
ADMISSION	:	Monday-Saturday 0930-1730 (1600 in winter); Sunday 1000-1800
FURTHER INFO	:	The aeronautical collection is spread around the museum which itself is one of the most comprehensive of its type in the world.

JUNKERS Ju-87B-1

COUNTRY OF ORIGIN	**RANGE**
Germany	490 miles (788 km)
ENGINES	**CEILING**
Junkers Jumo 211 12-cylinder V liquid-cooled 1,200 hp	26,250 ft (8,000 m)
CREW	**LENGTH**
	36 ft 5 in (11.10 m)
two	**SPAN**
MAX SPEED	45 ft 3 in (13.79 m)
238 mph (383 km/h) at 13,410 ft (4,090 m)	**HEIGHT**
	13 ft 2 in (4.01 m)

LOCKHEED F–80 SHOOTING STAR

The first jet-propelled combat aircraft to enter service with the USAF, the Shooting Star remained the workhorse of America's tactical fighter-bomber and fighter-interceptor squadrons for five years after the end of World War II, until it was replaced in 1950-51 by more modern types. The prototype flew on 9 January 1944, and in April 1945, two aircraft were shipped to Italy for evaluation under operational conditions, being the only US jet aircraft to see front-line service during the war. Apart from a few short day reconnaissance flights, they saw no action.

The Shooting Star entered service late in 1945 with the 412th Fighter Group. The major production version was the F-80C, and this was still first-line equipment in the summer of 1950, at the outbreak of the Korean War. It equipped six fighter and fighter-bomber groups, and one tactical reconnaissance squadron, in the Pacific area and Japan, and all rendered valuable service in the war, flying escort missions for B-29s as well as carrying out ground-attack missions on a large scale. The F-80s of the 35th Fighter-Bomber Squadron were the first to see combat, destroying four North Korean Ilyushin Il-10 bombers on 27 June 1950, and on 7 November F-80s of the 51st Fighter Interceptor Wing fought MiG-15s over the Yalu River in history's first jet-versus-jet battle, destroying one of them. With the arrival of Sabres in Korea the Shooting Stars relinquished their fighter role, and by July 1953 only the RF-80Cs of the 67th Tactical Reconnaissance Wing were operational in Korea.

ALAMOGORDO CITY PARK

OWNER/OPERATOR :	Alamogordo City Council
ADDRESS :	Alamogordo City Park, Alamogordo, New Mexico
LOCATION	
ADMISSION :	Free access
FURTHER INFO :	Alamogordo is 6 miles northeast of the large Holloman Air Force Base which is home to a number of both aircraft and missile units.

Above: The F-80 can also be seen at Robbins Air Force Base Museum of Aviation in Georgia.

LOCKHEED F-80C SHOOTING STAR

COUNTRY OF ORIGIN
USA

ENGINES
General Electric J33-A-23 turbojet, 4,600 lb (2,086 kg) thrust

CREW
one

MAX SPEED
580 mph (933 km/h) at 7,000 ft (2,133 m)

RANGE
1,380 miles (2,220 km)

CEILING
42,750 ft (13,030 m)

LENGTH
34 ft 6 in (10.51 m)

SPAN
39 ft 11 in (11.85 m)

HEIGHT
11 ft 4 in (3.45 m)

LOCKHEED T–33 SHOOTING STAR

The most widely used advanced trainer in the world, the Lockheed T-33 flew in 1948 and was developed from the F-80 Shooting Star. The type was designated T-33A in USAF service and T-33B (T2-V) with the US Navy and Marine Corps. It is estimated that some 90 per cent of the free world's military jet pilots trained on the T-33 during the 1950s and 1960s. About 5,700 T-33s were built in the USA alone, and others under licence in Canada and Japan. The US Navy's version, the T2-V, entered service in 1957 and featured extensive cockpit redesign. It was used as a deck landing and navigational trainer.

The T-33 served as the USAF's principal advanced trainer for three decades. After 500 hours of ground instruction, student pilots carried out 100 hours of basic flying training and then passed on to a further 75 hours in the T-33 before instruction on fighter aircraft. Although the T-33 has now been replaced in the advanced trainer role by the Cessna T-37, it is still widely used throughout the USAF, where it is familiarly known as the 'T-Bird'. About 200 T-33s are used for combat support, proficiency and radar target illumination training. Student navigators also trained on the T-33 before this task was taken over by the T-37.

LOCKHEED T-33A SHOOTING STAR	
COUNTRY OF ORIGIN	**RANGE**
USA	800 miles (1,280 km)
ENGINES	**CEILING**
5,400 lb (2,454 kg) thrust Allison J33-A35 turbojet	47,500 ft (14,481 m)
CREW	**LENGTH**
two	37 ft 9 in (11.50 m)
MAX SPEED	**SPAN**
600 mph (960 km/h)	42 ft 5 in (12.92 m)
	HEIGHT
	11 ft 8 in (3.55 m)

WAR MEMORIAL, GJIROKASTER		
ADDRESS	:	On the old city ramparts, Gjirokaster, Albania
LOCATION	:	Approx 90 miles (145 km) south east of the capital Tirana
ADMISSION	:	Daylight hours
FURTHER INFO	:	Precise information is difficult to obtain at the present time.

Above: The Shooting Star at the War Museum in Gjirokaster, Albania.
Below: An example on display at the McClellan Aviation Museum, Sacramento, California.

McDonnell F2H Banshee

O n 2 March 1945 the United States Navy placed a contract with the McDonnell Aircraft Corporation for two prototypes of a new naval fighter-bomber design, the XF2D-1. The first of these flew on 11 January 1947 and the first of 56 production F2H-1 Banshees was delivered to Navy Squadron VF-171 in March 1949. In August that year, Lt J L Fruin of VF-171 made the first use in the United States of an ejection seat in a real emergency, ejecting from a Banshee at a speed of over 500 knots.

The F2H-2 was an improved version with an uprated engine and more fuel tankage, and by the time the Korean War broke out in 1950, 334 of these were in service or on order. Operating with squadrons of Task Force 77, the Banshee went into action for the first time on 23 August 1951, when the F2H-2s of VF-172 (USS *Essex*) struck at targets in north-eastern Korea. Two days later, Banshees of the same unit undertook their first fighter escort mission, accompanying B-29s in a high-altitude bombing attack on North Korean marshalling yards at Rashin.

The F2H-3 (redesignated F2-C in 1962) was a long-range limited all-weather fighter development with a lengthened fuselage, also equipping two squadrons of the Royal Canadian Navy.

The Banshee was retired from first-line US Navy service in September 1959, the last unit to be equipped with it being VAW-11. The Canadian Navy's Banshees remained in service until the mid-1960s.

EL TORO MARINE CORPS AIR STATION	
OWNER/OPERATOR :	United States Marine Corps
ADDRESS :	El Toro, Santa Ana, California 92709
LOCATION :	5 miles east of Los Angeles. Road – Interstate 5
ADMISSION :	Some aircraft on permanent view
FURTHER INFO :	This major marine corps base is home to many units which operate a variety of types.

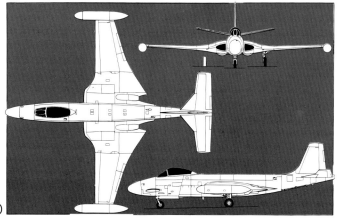

McDONNELL F2H-4 BANSHEE	
COUNTRY OF ORIGIN	
USA	
ENGINES	
two Westinghouse J34-WE-38 turbojets, 3,600 lb (1,633 kg) thrust each	
CREW	
one	
MAX SPEED	
532 mph (856 km/h) at 10,000 ft (3,048 m)	

RANGE	
1,475 miles (2,370 km)	
CEILING	
44,800 ft (13,650 m)	
LENGTH	
40 ft 2 in (12.25 m)	
SPAN	
44 ft 10 in (13.66 m)	
HEIGHT	
14 ft 6 in (4.42 m)	

MESSERSCHMITT ME 262

I n November 1943 Hitler's overruling command to the Luftwaffe forced them to order the bomber version of the Messerschmitt Me 262, rather than the fighter variant for which it was designed. The decision robbed the German air force of a potent – and much needed – weapon in the later stages of World War II. The Me 262 was Germany's and the world's first jet fighter, and had it been developed earlier, could have inflicted much greater losses to the Allied air forces.

The project had its origins in a request to Messerschmitt from the RLM (the German air ministry) to design a fighter to be powered by the new turbojet engines then under development. The early engines proved unsuitable, and the Me 262 did not fly until 19 July 1942 when the Junkers Jumo engine became available.

Given a very low development priority by the RLM, series production eventually commenced in 1944 as a fighter. Some two months later, Hitler discovered what had occurred, and ordered production to be switched to bombers, all completed airframes to be converted accordingly. Adding further delay and diffusion of effort, other variants were developed to operate in the all-weather fighter, photo-reconnaissance, night fighter and dual-control trainer roles.

As the war was reaching its conclusion, Hitler changed his mind and gave total priority of aircraft production to the Me 262A-1 fighter. It was too late; of some 1,400 Me 262s produced, no more than 100 saw operational service.

Main picture: The Me 262 at the Planes of Fame Air Museum.
Inset: Another example at the Wings of Freedom Air and Space Museum, Pennsylvania.

PLANES OF FAME AIR MUSEUM

OWNER/OPERATOR	:	Ed Maloney
ADDRESS	:	7000 Merrill Avenue, Chino Airport, California 91710
LOCATION	:	7 miles south of Ontario. Road – Route 83
ADMISSION	:	Daily 0900-1700
FURTHER INFO	:	Onee of the major Warbird Airfields in the USA, Chino holds a unique annual show and will hold any aviation buffs for many hours.

MESSERSCHMITT Me 262

COUNTRY OF ORIGIN	**RANGE**
Germany	682 miles (1,050 km)
ENGINES	**CEILING**
two Junkers Jumo 004B-1, 1,980 lb (898 kg) thrust	37,565 ft (11,450 m)
CREW	**LENGTH**
one	34 ft 9.5 in (10.60 m)
MAX SPEED	**SPAN**
540 mph (869 km/h) at 19,685 ft (6,000 m)	40 ft 11.5 in (12.48 m)
	HEIGHT
	12 ft 7 in (3.84 m)

MIKOYAN–GUREVICH MiG-15

Perhaps the most famous jet fighter produced by the Soviet Union, the MiG-15 saw service with the Soviet air force in the Korean War, where it was pitted against the USAF's F-86 Sabre.

Supplied to every Eastern Bloc air force, and many other countries around the world, the second generation MiG-15 had a long and distinguished career once a suitable power plant had been acquired. This occurred in 1946 when, under a new trade agreement and amid much criticism, the British government supplied the USSR with full details and examples of the Rolls-Royce Nene, at that time the world's most advanced jet engine.

The MiG-15 (known to NATO by the code name Fagot) first flew on 30 December 1947 and became operational the following year, remaining in service until the mid-1970s. Over 8,000 examples were produced, which did not include those produced under licence in Czechoslovakia, Poland and the Chinese Republic. In addition to the fighter variants, a tandem two-seat trainer was built in large numbers. Designated the MiG-15UTI (NATO code name Midget), it had the distinction of being the world's first swept-wing jet conversion trainer.

A Chinese-built example in the Military Museum in Peking is displayed in North Korean Air Force markings. It is interesting to note that nine kills are depicted on the side of the aircraft, denoted by red stars – exactly the same symbol used by the USAF pilots at the time to denote Soviet kills.

Two examples of the MiG-15 can be seen in Peking, at the Military Museum Right, *and at the Aeronautical Institute* Below

MIKOYAN–GUREVICH MiG-15
COUNTRY OF ORIGIN
USSR
ENGINES
RD-45F (Rolls-Royce Nene) turbojet, 5,005 lb (2,270 kg) thrust
CREW
one
MAX SPEED
664 mph (1,070 km/h) at 40,000 ft (12,000 m)
RANGE
1,220 miles (1,960 km)
CEILING
50,000 ft (15,200 m)
LENGTH
36 ft 3 in (11.05 m)
SPAN
33 ft 1 in (10.08 m)
HEIGHT
11 ft 2 in (3.40 m)

MIL MI-4

Known as 'Hound' under the NATO code-name system for Soviet aircraft, the Mi-4, designed by Mikhail L Mil, was similar to America's Sikorsky S-55 but larger. It entered service with the Soviet air force in the summer of 1953 and could carry 14 fully equipped troops. Cargoes of up to 3,500 lb in weight – a 76-mm anti-tank gun, for example – could be loaded into the fuselage through clamshell rear loading doors. Production of the Mi-4 ran into thousands, and the type saw service in many countries as an assault helicopter. Mi-4s serving with the Soviet airline, Aeroflot, were used extensively on internal air networks, and in government service the type was used, among other things, in support of Soviet scientific expeditions to the Arctic and other remote regions.

The Mi-4 was the first helicopter to be built in China, where it was known as the Z-5. It remained in production there for some 20 years, and about 1,000 were built. Some Z-5s were later converted to use the PT6T-6 Turbo Twin Pac engine, developed by Pratt & Whitney Aircraft of Canada.

During its career the Mi-4 established two payload and altitude records in its class. On 26 April 1956 test pilot Yuri Vinizki lifted a load of over 2,000 lb (1,000 kg) to an altitude of 19,958 ft (6,084 m), and on 26 March 1960 this was raised to 24,491 ft (7,466 m) with a similar payload.

VIETNAMESE AIR FORCE MUSEUM	
OWNER/OPERATOR :	Vietnamese Air Force
ADDRESS :	Ba'u Tang Quan, Chung Ithong Quan, Hanoi, Vietnam
LOCATION :	In the southern suburbs of the city
ADMISSION :	Daily
FURTHER INFO :	The aircraft are on display outside the museum, which contains numerous artefacts, models, etc about the Vietnamese military campaigns.

Main picture: The Mil MI-4 at the Indian Air Force Museum.
Inset: On display at the Vietnamese Air Force Museum.

MIL Mi-4 ('HOUND')
COUNTRY OF ORIGIN
USSR
ENGINES
one Shvetsov ASh-82V 14-cylinder air-cooled radial rated at 1,700 hp for take-off and 1,430 hp maximum continuous rating
CREW
two
MAX SPEED
155 mph (248 km/h)
RANGE
248 miles (396 km)
CEILING
16,000 ft (4,878 m)
LENGTH
53 ft 5 in (16.27 m)
ROTOR DIAMETER
56 ft 6 in (17.22 m)
HEIGHT
17 ft 0 in (5.18 m)

NORTH AMERICAN B25 MITCHELL

The B-25 design was so promising from the outset that the aircraft was ordered into production for the US Army Air Corps (as it was then) without any prototypes being built. The first one flew on 19 August 1940 and 24 had been delivered by the end of the year. These were followed by 40 B-25As, then 119 B-25Bs with dorsal and ventral gun turrets. The first unit to equip with the new bomber was the 17th Bombardment Group.

Production continued with 1,619 B-25Cs and 2,290 B-25Ds, starting early in 1942, and in April that year a formation of Mitchells, flying from the carrier USS *Hornet* and led by Major (later General) James Doolittle, made an historic bombing raid on Tokyo. The B-25G and B-25H were heavily armed 'gunship'

versions, mounting a 75-mm cannon and up to 14 machine guns, and these wrought considerable havoc on Japanese shipping in the Pacific War.

The RAF also received 538 Mitchell IIs (B-25Cs and Ds) which equipped a number of bomber squadrons, mostly in Bomber Command's 2 Group. The Soviet Union received 870 Mitchells under Lend-Lease, while others were supplied to Brazil, China and the Netherlands. Some of the latter aircraft were taken over by the Republic of Indonesia and, during the period of confrontation with Malaysia in the early 1960s, carried out leaflet-dropping operations over North Borneo.

The main version of the Mitchell was the B-25J, and a total of 4,318 were completed.

INDONESIAN ARMED FORCES MUSEUM	
ADDRESS	: Jalan Gatot Subroto, Jakarta, Indonesia
LOCATION	: Between Jakarta and Halim Airport
ADMISSION	: Daily 1000-1700
FURTHER INFO	: The aircraft are situated in a park which also contains military vehicles on display.

The Mitchell can be seen around the world. *Top*: In North Weald, Essex, in the UK. *Centre*: On display at Jakarta Armed Forces Museum. *Bottom*: At the Marine Corps Air Ground Museum, Quantico, Virginia.

NORTH AMERICAN B-25H MITCHELL
COUNTRY OF ORIGIN
USA
ENGINES
two Wright R-2600-113 Cyclone 14-cylinder radial air-cooled, 1,700 hp each
CREW
five
MAX SPEED
275 mph (442 km/h) at 13,000 ft (3,960 m)
RANGE
1,350 miles (2,170 km)
CEILING
23,800 ft (7,250 m)
LENGTH
51 ft 0 in (15.54 m)
SPAN
67 ft 7 in (20.60 m)
HEIGHT
15 ft 9 in (4.80 m)

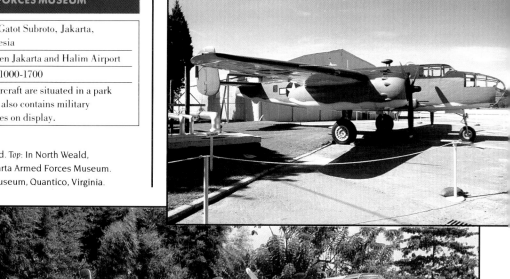

NORTH AMERICAN P51 MUSTANG

After a speedy, but less than dramatic, start to life in response to an urgent UK requirement for an advanced fighter, the North American Mustang developed into what was arguably the most versatile single-seat fighter of World War II.

In April 1940, the British Purchasing Commission gave North American just 120 days to deliver their proposal in prototype form, which they did with three days to spare. Unfortunately, the lack of a suitable engine delayed the programme and the first aircraft did not fly until 26 October 1940.

While early models were put into service as fighter-reconnaissance machines because of their poor engine performance at higher altitudes, the installation of the American-built Packard Merlin put the Mustang in a class of its own. In their re-engined form, some 1,800 Mustang III and IV were delivered to the RAF for fighter duties, while the USAAF used its ultra-long-range P-51C and P-51D machines as escorts for its daylight bomber formations.

The RAF's Mustangs were withdrawn by the end of 1946, coinciding with the end of a production run of 15,576 aircraft. However, proving that you can't keep a good one down, the P-51 was re-engined with a Rolls-Royce Dart turboprop by Cavalier Aircraft Corp in 1967 as a low-budget performance aircraft, supplying to third-world nations under the United State's Mutual Aid Program.

The fourth prototype XP-51A was seconded to become the first in service with the USAAF for evaluation purposes. Later stored by the National Air and Space Museum, it was acquired by the EAA Foundation with whom it was restored and regularly flown until August, 1982. It now has pride of place in the Warbirds section of their Oshkosh museum.

NORTH AMERICAN P-51 MUSTANG	
COUNTRY OF ORIGIN	**RANGE**
USA	1,710 miles (2,736 km)
ENGINES	**CEILING**
one 1,695 hp Packard Merlin V-1650-7	n/a
CREW	**LENGTH**
one	32 ft 3 in (10.50 m)
MAX SPEED	**SPAN**
442 mph (707 km/h)	37 ft 0.3 in (11.90 m)
	HEIGHT
	8 ft 8 in (2.63 m)

EXPERIMENTAL AIRCRAFT ASSOCIATION MUSEUM

OWNER/OPERATOR	:	The Experimental Aircraft Association
ADDRESS	:	3000 Poberezny Road, Wittman Field, Oshkosh, Wisconsin 54903
LOCATION	:	2 miles south of the city
ADMISSION	:	Daily 0830-1700 (Sunday opening 1100)
FURTHER INFO	:	The largest collection of homebuilt aircraft in the world, the museum also features warbirds, aerobatic and air racing aircraft. The 'Pioneer Airport' is a reconstruction of an airfield of the inter-war period.

Main picture: The Mustang at Fort Lauderdale, Florida, in the collection of the Whittington Brothers.
Inset: At the Experimental Aircraft Association in Wisconsin.

NORTH AMERICAN F86 SABRE

Blooded during the Korean conflict, the scene of the first large-scale air warfare between jet-powered aircraft, the North American F-86 Sabre was the first swept-wing jet fighter operated by the United States Air Force.

Considered the best fighter aircraft of its time, the Sabre out-flew and outfought the Russian MiG-15 over Korea even when outnumbered. Fast and very manoeuvrable, it was used by virtually all Western air forces, either new off the production lines or refurbished, and remained in front-line service for over 20 years.

Among its other distinctions, the Sabre became the first aircraft to be adopted as a standard design by NATO. As the F-86K, it was supplied to the air forces of Italy, France, West Germany, the Netherlands and Norway, many of the aircraft being built under licence by Fiat in Italy. Such was the demand for the Sabre that 1,815 were built by Canadair in Canada while others were constructed in Australia and Japan.

While design work started in 1944, the radical concept of a swept wing was not accepted until after the war when German research material had been studied, indicating that it significantly improved high speed performance.

The first prototype, the XF-86, made its maiden flight on 1 October 1947 and the Sabre entered service as the F-86A in February 1949.

Among the many Sabres preserved, an early F-86A is on display at the Selfridge Military Aircraft Museum, Michigan. One of the oldest air bases in the United States, it was named after Lt Thomas Selfridge who, killed in a flying accident with Orville Wright, became the first fatality in powered flight.

SELFRIDGE MILITARY AIR MUSEUM		
OWNER/OPERATOR	:	Michigan Air Guard Historical Association
ADDRESS	:	Selfridge Air Base, Michigan 48045
LOCATION	:	25 miles northeast of Detroit. Road – Interstate 94
ADMISSION	:	April-October Sundays 1300-1700
FURTHER INFO	:	The aircraft are parked outdoors alongside a small indoor exhibition which traces the history of the airfield.

Main picture: The Sabre at the Selfridge Military Museum.
Inset: At the George Air Force Base in California.

NORTH AMERICAN F-86D SABRE
COUNTRY OF ORIGIN
USA
ENGINES
General Electric J47-GE-17B turbojet, 7,500 lb (3,402 kg) thrust
CREW
one
MAX SPEED
692 mph (1,113 km/h)
RANGE
850 miles (1,378 km)
CEILING
50,000 ft (15,240 m)
LENGTH
40 ft 11 in (12.47 m)
SPAN
39 ft 1 in (11.91 m)
HEIGHT
14 ft 8 in (4.47 m)

NORTH AMERICAN XB70 VALKYRIE

he futuristic lines of the North American XB-70 Valkyrie belie the fact that it was designed in the early 1960s as a replacement for the Boeing B-52 strategic bomber. In practice, military thinking at the time was directed towards using intercontinental ballistic missiles in the role and as a result only two prototypes were built.

Unparalleled as the largest and most complex research aircraft ever built, the prototype XB-70A made its maiden flight on 21 September 1964. Originally designed to fly up to 7,600 miles (12,230 km) unrefuelled, at a constant speed in excess of Mach 3, it incorporated both unusual design features and materials.

Featuring a canard delta wing arrangement, the Valkyrie had a long slim titanium fuselage above the wing, and a broad rectangular engine nacelle beneath. A unique feature was the wing design whereby the outer sections hinged down 25 degrees for low-level supersonic flight and 65 degrees for Mach 3 flights at high-altitude.

Virtually all of the test flying was undertaken by the first prototype. Early in the test programme, the second prototype was lost when it collided with a F-104 Starfighter photographic chase aircraft on 8 June 1966 with the loss of both crews.

Having reached a top speed of Mach 3.08 and altitude of 73,980 ft (22,550 m), the XB-70A Valkyrie made its last flight on 4 February 1969.

UNITED STATES AIR FORCE MUSEUM	
OWNER/OPERATOR :	United States Air Force
ADDRESS :	Wright Patterson Air Force Base, Dayton, Ohio 45433
LOCATION :	4 miles northeast of Dayton. Road – Highway 4
ADMISSION :	Monday-Friday 0900-1700 (annex 0930-1500) Saturday-Sunday 1000-1800 (annex 1030-1700)
FURTHER INFO :	The museum has the largest collection of aircraft in the world, although many aircraft are loaned to other museums in the USA and abroad and therefore not on show.

NORTH AMERICAN XB-70A VALKYRIE
COUNTRY OF ORIGIN
USA
ENGINES
six General Electric YN93-GE-3 turbojets, 31,000 lb (14,060 kg) thrust (with afterburning each)
CREW
two
MAX SPEED
mach 3
RANGE
7,600 miles (12,230 km)
CEILING
73,980 ft (22,550 m)
LENGTH
196 ft 0 in (59.64 m)
SPAN
105 ft 0 in (32 m) tips spread
HEIGHT
30 ft 0 in (9.14 m)

PZL P–11

When Poland's State Aviation Works was founded in Warsaw at the end of 1927, designer Ing Zygmunt Pulawski set to work on a series of outstanding monoplane fighters featuring a high-set strut-braced gull wing which allowed the pilot a perfect view for air combat. This concept reached its acme in the P-11, powered by the licence-built Bristol Mercury radial engine. The first prototype of this attractive fighter made its maiden flight in September 1931, powered by a Bristol Jupiter. The first production batch, comprising 30 aircraft, was completed in one year — 1934 — and total P-11 production ran to 250 units.

The P-11's fuselage was a stressed-skin duralumin structure, while the wing had a duralumin framework and was mostly covered with corrugated duralumin sheet. The long, narrow-chord ailerons could double as flaps to reduce landing speeds. The v-strutted fixed landing gear was exceptionally strong. Basic armament was a pair of 0.3 calibre KM Wz33 machine guns with 500 rounds each, fitted in the fuselage sides and firing through the propeller arc.

On September 1 1939, when Hitler's invading forces swept into Poland, the Polish Air Force was outnumbered nine to one by the Luftwaffe, whose equipment was far superior. Nonetheless, the Polish Air Force put up dogged resistance for 17 days, losing 333 of its 430 front-line aircraft. At the forefront of this desperate battle was the P-11C, now obsolete but highly manoeuvrable and flown by courageous pilots. Despite heroic efforts, the superior force prevailed, and on September 17 the remaining 38 P-11s and P-7s (an earlier type) were evacuated to Rumania.

MUZEUM LOTNICTURA I ASTRONAUTYKI		
ADDRESS	:	30-969 Krakov 28, Poland
LOCATION	:	3 miles east of the city at the disused Rakowice airfield. Road – Route E22
ADMISSION	:	May-October 1000-1400
FURTHER INFO	:	The museum includes the survivors from the famous Deutsche Luftfahrtsammlung (Berlin Air Museum) which was destroyed in an air raid.

PZL P-11	
COUNTRY OF ORIGIN	Poland
ENGINES	Gnome-Rhone 14 N7 14-cylinder radial air-cooled 930 hp
CREW	one
MAX SPEED	254 mph (408 km/h) at 14,763 ft (4,490 m)
RANGE	497 miles (800 km)
CEILING	29,527 ft (9,000 m)
LENGTH	24 ft 7.5 in (7.52 m)
SPAN	35 ft 2 in (10.75 m)
HEIGHT	8 ft 10 in (2.70 m)

REPUBLIC P47 THUNDERBOLT

nquestionably one of the great fighters of World War II, the 'Jug', as it was affectionately known, was designed by Alexander Kartveli to meet a United States Army Air Force requirement for a 'super fighter'. It first flew on 6 May, 1941 as the XP-47B, a rotund six-ton giant of a fighter spanning 40 ft and powered by a supercharged 2,000 hp Pratt & Whitney radial engine.

Although the Thunderbolt had none of the sleek elegance of its European counterparts, it soon proved to be an agile and doughty opponent.

Under the pressures of war, development proceeded apace. The P-47C, which appeared late in 1942, could carry a ventral fuel tank and also had increased internal fuel capacity to increase the type's range. In combat over Europe, the Thunderbolt soon began to give a good account of itself, providing valuable service as a bomber escort.

In 1943 the P-47D came into service, this development having water injection to coax another 300 hp from the engine, and paddle-bladed propellers. To improve all-round visibility, a bubble canopy was introduced on later P-47Ds; the rear fuselage top-decking was cut down to accommodate this. Later in the year the Thunderbolt came to be used as a fighter-bomber – a role in which it excelled.

The 'Jug' subsequently served in nearly all of the war theatres, and served with the RAF, the Free French and the Russians. The ultimate version was the long-range P-47N, with redesigned wings, for service in the Pacific theatre. Production of all variants totalled 15,683 aircraft, and P-47s were credited with the destruction of more than 7,000 enemy aircraft, 3,753 of these in aerial combat.

NEW ENGLAND AIR MUSEUM	
OWNER/OPERATOR :	Connecticut Aeronautical Historical Association
ADDRESS :	Bradley International Airport, Windsor Locks, Connecticut 06096
LOCATION :	North side of the airport. Road – Route 75
ADMISSION :	Daily 1000-1700
FURTHER INFO :	Approximately 40 aircraft are displayed in the exhibition hall of the museum which is becoming one of the major aviation museums in the USA.

Left: The Thunderbolt at the New England Air Museum.

Below: Another example at the Lone Star Flight Museum in Houston, Texas.

REPUBLIC P-47D THUNDERBOLT
COUNTRY OF ORIGIN
USA
ENGINES
Pratt & Whitney R-2800-59 double Wasp 18-cylinder radial air-cooled, 2,535 hp
CREW
one
MAX SPEED
428 mph (689 km/h) at 30,000 ft (9,150 m)
RANGE
475 miles (765 km)
CEILING
42,000 ft (12,800 m)
LENGTH
36 ft 2 in (11 m)
SPAN
40 ft 9 in (14.42 m)
HEIGHT
14 ft 2 in (4.31 m)

SIKORSKY S-58

n June 1952 the United States Navy ordered a new anti-submarine helicopter from Sikorsky Aircraft. The helicopter was given the manufacturer's designation S-58, and the US Navy designation XHSS-1. The prototype made its maiden flight on 8 March 1954, heralding a long production run of more than 2,250 aircraft by Sikorsky alone.

The S-58 was powered by a 1,525 hp Wright R-1820 radial piston engine, mounted obliquely in the nose. This allowed the transmission shaft to run at right angles to the engine, straight into the gearbox beneath the hub of the four-bladed main rotor. To facilitate stowage on board ship, the rotor blades could be folded aft, while the rear fuselage and tail rotor folded forward.

The majority of S-58s were built for military use, but the type also served as a commercial transport, carrying up to 18 passengers. Operators included Sabena and Chicago Helicopter Airways. The 350 S-58s supplied to the US Navy were originally designated HSS Seabat, and the 603 built for the US Marines were HUS Seahorse. Later, both were redesignated H-34, this identity covering a range of variants developed for specific tasks.

The US Army also ordered the S-58, and the H-34 Choctaw soon became the Service's principal transport helicopter. Other nations which equipped their forces with the S-58 included Japan and West Germany, while 135 were built under licence by Aerospatiale of France and 365 by Westland in Great Britain. These served with the Royal Navy as the Wessex, also doing duty with the Royal Marines and Royal Air Force. The Wessex had a 1,450 hp Napier Gazelle turbine in place of the S-58's Wright radial.

The S-58 undertook many other duties, such as search and rescue, casualty evacuation, support and ground attack, and even VIP transport.

SIKORSKY S-58		
COUNTRY OF ORIGIN	**RANGE**	
USA	384 miles (614 km)	
ENGINES	**CEILING**	
one 1,525 hp Wright R-1820-84 piston-engine	4,000 ft (1,219 m)	
CREW	**LENGTH**	
two	47 ft 2 in (14.37 m)	
MAX SPEED	**ROTOR DIAMETER**	
123 mph (196 km/h)	56 ft 0 in (17.07 m)	
	HEIGHT	
	15 ft 10 in (4.75 m)	

LUFTWAFFEN MUSEUM	
OWNER/OPERATOR :	Luftwaffe
ADDRESS :	Fliegerhorst Uetersen, Uetersen 2082, Germany
LOCATION :	20 km northwest of Hamburg. Roads – between Roads no 5 and no 431
ADMISSION :	Daily – but check first
FURTHER INFO :	The museum is in two hangars on the north side of this non-flying military base. It traces the history of the Luftwaffe up to the present day.

Main picture: The Sikorsky S-58 in the Luftwaffe Museum. *Inset*: Civilian Wessex disguised as a US Marine S-58 at the International Helicopter Museum, Avon.

Sud–Ouest S.O.4050 Vautour

The Vautour (Vulture) was the product of designer Jean Charles Parot and his team at SNCA de Sud-Ouest, designed to meet a 1951 French Air Staff specification for a versatile twin-jet aircraft which could be used in the all-weather fighter, close support, light bomber, and reconnaissance roles. With its 35° swept wing, underslung SNECMA Atar turbojets, tandem twin-wheel main undercarriage and stabilizing auxiliary wheels housed in the engine nacelles, it was a distinctive and advanced machine for its time.

The first prototype, configured as a two-seat night fighter, made its maiden flight on 16 October 1952 and later exceeded the speed of sound in a shallow dive. The second prototype, a single-seat ground-attack aircraft, flew on December 4 1953, and the third, the bomber variant, flew a year later. The French Air Staff ordered 300 Vautour IIA single-seat attack aircraft, 140 Vautour IIN night and all-weather fighters, and 40 Vautour IIB bombers. The IIAs were cancelled in 1957, only 30 being flown, and 25 were sold to Israel in 1960; only 70 IINs were built, these being delivered to the Armée de l'Air in 1956-59; all 40 IIBs were produced and formed the nucleus of the Armée de l'Air's deterrent force, the Commandement des Forces Aériennes Strategiques. The final Vautour variant, the IIBR bomber-reconnaissance aircraft, did not go into production.

The last Vautours in service in France were the II.1Ns of the 30e Escadre at Reims, which were replaced by Mirage F1.Cs in the mid-1970s. The Israeli IIAs were withdrawn from combat duty after the October 1973 war, some being converted to carry electronic countermeasures.

BASE AERIENNE REIMS	
OWNER/OPERATOR :	L'Armée de l'Air
ADDRESS :	Reims/Champagne Base Aerienne, Reims, France
LOCATION :	4 miles (6 km) north of Reims
ADMISSION :	On view at entrance
FURTHER INFO :	Reims/Champagne is an operational French Air Force base.

SUD-OUEST S.O. VAUTOUR	
COUNTRY OF ORIGIN	**RANGE**
France	3,728 miles (5,964 km)
ENGINES	**CEILING**
two 7,716 lb st (3,506 kg) SNECMA Atar turbojets	44,290 ft (13,503 m)
CREW	**LENGTH**
one/two	51 ft 1 in (15.56 m)
MAX SPEED	**SPAN**
720 mph (1,152 km/h)	49 ft 6.5 in (15.09 m)
	HEIGHT
	14 ft 1 in (4. 26 m)

SUPERMARINE SPITFIRE

No aircraft in the history of aviation has stirred the imagination as much as the Supermarine Spitfire. The symbol of the superiority of the Royal Air Force over the might of the German Luftwaffe during the Battle of Britain, the Spitfire was a thoroughbred classic aeroplane. Designed to the same Air Ministry specification as the Hawker Hurricane, it incorporated many design features from the Supermarine S-6B seaplane which had won the Schneider Trophy outright for Britain.

While both companies' designs adequately met the specifications, the two chief designers looked at the requirements from completely different angles. It has been said that, while Sydney Camm of Hawker produced a solid war-horse capable of taking considerable punishment, Supermarine's Mitchell designed a ballerina.

ISRAELI AIR FORCE HISTORIC COLLECTION	
OWNER/OPERATOR :	Israeli Air Force
ADDRESS :	Hatzerim Air Force Base, Neger, Israel
LOCATION :	South of Beersheba
ADMISSION :	Stricly prior permission only
FURTHER INFO :	Hatzerim AFB is home of the Israeli Air Force's flying school which operates both fixed and rotary wing aircraft.

Below right: The Spitfire can also be seen at the Imperial War Museum in London.

SUPERMARINE SPITFIRE MK 1
COUNTRY OF ORIGIN
UK
ENGINES
Rolls-Royce Merlin II 12-cylinder V liquid-cooled, 1,030 hp
CREW
one
MAX SPEED
355 mph (571 km/h) at 19,000 ft (5,800 m)
RANGE
500 miles (805 km)
CEILING
34,000 ft (10,360 m)
LENGTH
29 ft 11 in (9.12 m)
SPAN
36 ft 10 in (11.22 m)
HEIGHT
11 ft 5 in (3.48 m)

The history of the Spitfire has been well documented, and requires little repetition. It fought in virtually every theatre of World War II, and remained in military service into the 1960s. From entering service in 1938, the design was constantly developed so that by the time production ended in October 1947, 20,351 aircraft in some 40 different variants had been produced — more than any other British aircraft type.

A relatively large number of Spitfires survive, and many are being rebuilt to flying condition. An interesting example is the 'Black Spitfire', former personal mount of Ezer Wiezman, chief of the Israel air force, which is still in flying condition. Now preserved at the IAF museum at Beersheba, it was previously with the Czech Air Force.

TACHIKAWA KI-36

A requirement for a two-seat, single-engined army co-operation monoplane was issued by the Japanese military authorities in 1937. It was to be extremely manoeuvrable at low altitudes, and able to operate from rough airstrips close to the front line. Radio and photographic equipment, and racks for light anti-personnel bombs were to be carried.

Two designs tendered to the specification were duly considered, and Tachikawa Hikoki KK was instructed to build prototypes of its proposal, the Ki-36, designed under the leadership of Ryokichi Endo. The Ki-36 was a low-wing, radial-engined monoplane with a fixed, spatted undercarriage. The swept-back leading edge of its wing allowed the pilot a good forward and downward view, and transparent panels were in the wing centre section beneath the fuselage.

The first Ki-36 prototype made its maiden flight on 20 April 1938, at Tachikawa, and proved to have a brisk take-off and a sprightful performance. Armament comprised a single forward-firing 7.7 mm Type 89 machine gun within the engine cowling, and a similar weapon on a movable mounting.

Production started in November 1938, the aircraft being known as the Army Type 98 Direct Co-operation Plane. During the second Sino-Japanese conflict, Ki-36s were used with success in small detachments assigned to Japanese Army units. In the Pacific in World War II, however, they were out-classed by Allied fighters and were relegated to China. Thailand took delivery of a small number of Ki-36s, the example depicted being one of these.

Above: The Tachikawa Ki-36 at the Royal Thai Air Force Museum. An example of the Ki-55 (right) is at the Peking Military Museum.

ROYAL THAI AIR FORCE MUSEUM	
OWNER/OPERATOR :	Royal Thai Air Force
ADDRESS :	Don Muang Air Force Base, Bangkok, Thailand
LOCATION :	15 miles northeast of the city on the Polyothin Road
ADMISSION :	Monday-Friday 0830-1630 (Closed 1200-1300). First weekend in the month 0900-1700 (closed 1200-1400)
FURTHER INFO :	The museum is perhaps the most important aviation collection in Asia. It houses a comprehensive display of models and memorabilia while the aircraft are restored to a high standard.

TACHIKAWA KI-36	
COUNTRY OF ORIGIN	**RANGE**
Japan	767 miles (1,235 km)
ENGINES	**CEILING**
one 450 hp Hitachi HA-13 air-cooled radial	26,700 ft (8,277 m)
CREW	**LENGTH**
two	26 ft 3 in (8.00 m)
MAX SPEED	**SPAN**
216 mph (348 km/h)	38 ft 8.5 in (11.80 m)
	HEIGHT
	11 ft 11.5 in (3.64 m)

TUPOLEV TU-2

In 1938, the Soviet collective headed by Andrei N Tupolev designed the ANT-58 to meet an official specification for a sturdy twin-engined bomber able to carry a crew of three plus a 4,410 lb (2,000 kg) bomb load, and capable of level and diving attacks. An attractive mid-wing monoplane with twin fins and rudders, the ANT-58 first flew on 29 January 1941. Despite problems with its 1,400 hp AM-37 engines, the bomber had an exceptional performance, and development proceeded through two further prototypes, the four-seater ANT-59 and ANT-60, the latter having M-82 (later ASh-82) radials.

In 1942 work was started on a pre-production series of aircraft under the official designation Tu-2, and three of these first saw action later that year. The new bomber, which had excellent handling characteristics, was received enthusiastically, and after extensive structural modification to simplify construction it went into full production as the Tu-2S, with 1,850 hp M-82FN engines. Quantity deliveries began early in 1944. By the end of the war in Europe, 1,111 had been built.

Development continued during and after the war, with various engine and armament installations being tested. Photographic reconnaissance, torpedo-bomber and ground-attack variants were also produced.

Production of the basic Tu-2 continued until 1947, when 3,000 had been delivered to the Soviet Air Force, China, Poland, and other Communist countries. Later aircraft were

MUZEUM WOJSKA POLSKIEGO

OWNER/OPERATOR	:	Polish Army
ADDRESS	:	Al Jerozolimskie 3, Warszawa 00-950, Poland
LOCATION	:	In Warsaw city centre near the river Vistula
ADMISSION	:	Daily: Monday, Thursday, Saturday 1200-1700; Wednesday 1300-1900; Friday 1000-1500; Sunday 1030-1700
FURTHER INFO	:	The army museum in fact covers the history of all the Polish armed forces. In addition to a large collection of military vehicles and artillery items, the museum has a number of Russian military aircraft on display.

powered by ASh-82FNV engines driving four-bladed airscrews. A lighter training development, the UTB, was developed by Sukhoi, and a number of these were supplied to the Polish Air Force.

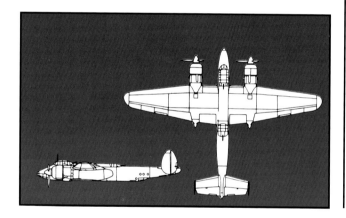

TUPOLEV Tu-2		
COUNTRY OF ORIGIN		
USSR		
ENGINES		
two Shvestov M-82 14-cylinder radial air-cooled, 1,850 hp each		
CREW		
four		
MAX SPEED		
342 mph (550 km/h) at 17,720 ft (5,400 m)		

RANGE	
1,243 miles (2,000 km)	
CEILING	
31,200 ft (9,500 m)	
LENGTH	
45 ft 3 in (13.80 m)	
SPAN	
61 ft 10.5 in (18.85 m)	
HEIGHT	
13 ft 11 in (4.25 m)	

VOUGHT F4U CORSAIR

he Corsair ranks as one of the truly great fighters of World War II, and remained in production longer than any other US fighter of that war. In response to a 1938 requirement for a single-seat shipboard fighter, Vought designer Rex Beisel took the most powerful engine available and built the smallest possible airframe around it. To keep the undercarriage short despite the large-diameter propeller, the aircraft was given its distinctive inverted gull wing, with the main legs located at the lowest point.

The XF4U-1 prototype first took to the air on 29 May 1940, powered by a 2,000 hp Pratt & Whitney Double Wasp. It proved to be faster than any US fighter then flying, and was ordered into production, deliveries of the F4U-1 beginning in October 1942. As well as serving with the US Marines and Navy, Corsairs were supplied to Britain's Royal Navy under Lend-Lease, and also to the Royal New Zealand Air Force. Fleet Air Arm Corsairs based in HMS *Victorious* saw action on 3 April 1944, during the attacks on the *Tirpitz*. In the Pacific theatre the Corsair quickly demonstrated its superiority over its Japanese opponents; Marine Corps F4Us destroyed no fewer than 584 enemy aircraft by the end of 1943.

There was a range of developments and variants to suit specific roles, and even the end of the war failed to stop Corsair production. The XF4U-6, redesignated AU-1, served with the Marines in Korea, and the final variant, the F4U-7, was used by the US Navy and also by the Aéronavale, with whom it served in Indochina. Production ended in December 1952.

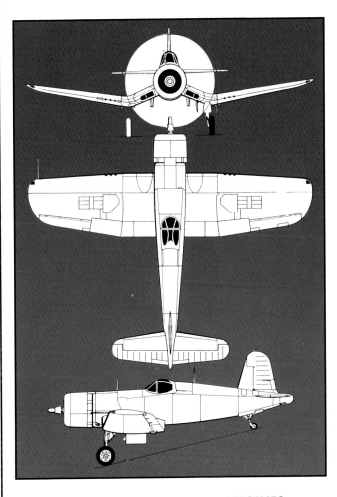

THE AIR MUSEUM – PLANES OF FAME EAST		
OWNER/OPERATOR	:	Bob Pond
ADDRESS	:	14771 Pioneer Trail, Eden Prairie, Minnesota 55344
LOCATION	:	Flying Cloud Airport, 12 miles southeast of Minneapolis. Road – County Road 1
ADMISSION	:	May-September 1100-1700 Saturday-Sunday or by appointment
FURTHER INFO	:	In the words of aviation museum specialist Bob Ogden, 'The fine condition of the aircraft and the nature of their surroundings makes this collection one of the most impressive in the USA'.

VOUGHT F4U-1D CORSAIR	
COUNTRY OF ORIGIN	
USA	
ENGINES	Pratt & Whitney R-2800-8W double Wasp 18-cylinder radial air-cooled, 2,000 hp
CREW	one
MAX SPEED	425 mph (684 km/h) at 20,000 ft (6,100 m)
RANGE	1,015 miles (1,635 km)
CEILING	37,000 ft (11,280 m)
LENGTH	33 ft 4.5 in (10.16 m)
SPAN	41 ft (12.47 m)
HEIGHT	15 ft 1 in (4.60 m)

WESTLAND WYVERN

A single-seat carrier-borne strike aircraft, the Wyvern was designed from the outset to be powered by a propeller turbine. However, because such engines did not become available until 1948, the first examples, designated Wyvern T.F.1, had 2,690 hp Rolls-Royce Eagle piston engines. The first prototype Wyvern made its maiden flight on 16 December 1946, and the example which survives today in the Fleet Air Arm Museum, VR137, is one of seven 'production' T.F.1s. These aircraft were soon succeeded by the Wyvern T.F.2, the first turbine-powered variant, which flew in 1949. One of these had a Rolls-Royce Clyde engine, but the remainder were fitted with the Armstrong Siddeley Python. Thirteen of the 20 ordered were delivered, but the remaining seven were converted to S.4 standard.

The Wyvern S.4, which made its maiden flight in May 1951, was the first variant to reach operational status, seven years after the first Wyvern had flown. This delay was attributable to development problems with the aircraft and its new and untried engines, which led to the loss of several aircraft and test pilots. The S.4 entered service with 813 Squadron, Fleet Air Arm, in May 1953, and first went to sea in HMS *Albion*, in 1954. The type equipped four first-line squadrons, the others being Nos 827, 830 and 831, but No 830, in HMS *Eagle*, was the only unit to fly its Wyverns operationally, using them for ground-attack sorties on Dekheila and Port Said during the Anglo-French intervention in Egypt in November 1956. The last Wyverns were withdrawn from service in March 1958, when 813 Squadron was disbanded at Royal Naval Air Station Ford, Sussex.

THE FLEET AIR ARM MUSEUM

OWNER/OPERATOR	:	The Royal Navy
ADDRESS	:	Royal Naval Air Station, Yeovilton, Ilchester, Somerset BA22 8HT
LOCATION	:	2 miles east of Ilchester. Road – B3151
ADMISSION	:	Daily 1000-1730 (or dusk if earlier)
FURTHER INFO	:	One of the important military aircraft collections in the world, the museum is also home to the Concorde exhibition which features the British prototype 002.

WESTLAND WYVERN S.4

COUNTRY OF ORIGIN	**RANGE**
UK	904 miles (1,455 km)
ENGINES	**CEILING**
Armstrong Siddeley Python ASP3 turboprop 4,110 hp	28,000 ft (8,535 m)
CREW	**LENGTH**
one	42 ft 3 in (12.87 m)
MAX SPEED	**SPAN**
383 mph (606 km/h) at sea level	44 ft 0 in (13.41 m)
	HEIGHT
	15 ft 9 in (4.80 m)

YAKOVLEV YAK–11

A two-seat intermediate trainer, the Yak-11 began to enter service with the Soviet Military Aviation Forces in 1947. Its wing planform bore a strong resemblance to that of the earlier Yak-3 and Yak-9 piston-engined fighters, but while they had been powered by well-streamlined liquid-cooled engines, the Yak-11's nose was blunt and housed a Shvetsov ASh-21 seven-cylinder air-cooled radial rated at 730 hp for take-off. The aircraft was of all-metal construction with fabric-covered control surfaces, and for gunnery training, a 7.7 mm machine gun was installed over the port side of the engine. The instructor and pupil were seated in tandem under a single canopy.

The West was unaware of the Yak-11's existence until March 1948, when one was accidentally crash-landed in Turkey, but its outstanding performance was revealed in 1950, when it set a number of FAI-homolgated records in its class, including a 500 m closed-circuit speed of 292.85 mph, a 1,000 km closed-circuit speed of 274.76 mph, a 2,000 km closed-circuit speed of 223.69 mph, and a distance recorded in a straight line of 1,236.64 miles.

Thousands of Yak-11s were built in the Soviet Union and under licence in other Communist countries, and it became one of the world's most widely-used trainers, serving with the air arms of 15 nations, including Albania, Austria, Afghanistan, Bulgaria, China, Czechoslovakia, Egypt, Hungary, Poland, Rumania, Syria and the Yemen. Four were presented to the Austrian Air Force by the Soviet government. Several Yak-11s are now flying in the West. The example depicted belongs to an American private owner.

ROBERT F YANCY COLLECTION

OWNER/OPERATOR	:	Robert F Yancy
ADDRESS	:	Klamath Falls, Oregon, USA
ADMISSION	:	Prior permission only
FURTHER INFO	:	The aircraft can be seen at major air races in the United States, especially Reno.

YAKOVLEV Yak-11

COUNTRY OF ORIGIN	RANGE
USSR	720 miles (1,152 km)
ENGINES	**CEILING**
one 730 hp Shvetsov ASh-21	24,600 ft (7,500 m)
CREW	**LENGTH**
two	27 ft 11 in (8.50 m)
	SPAN
	30 ft 10 in (9.40 m)
MAX SPEED	**HEIGHT**
295 mph (472 km/h)	6 ft 6 in (1.95 m)

MAJOR COLLECTIONS

UNITED STATES

Aerospace Museum, Hampton, VA
Castle Air Museum, Castle AFB, Atwater, CA
Champlin Fighter Museum, Mesa, AZ
Chanute Air Force Base, Chanute AFB, Rantoul, IL
Combat Jets Flying Museum, Houston, TX
Confederate Air Force (Pacific Wing), Madera, CA
Confederate Air Force, Mesa, AZ
Cradle of Aviation Museum, Garden City, NJ
El Toro Marine Corps Air Station, Santa Ana, CA
Evergreen Air Services, Marana, TX
Experimental Aircraft Association Museum, Oshkosh, WI
Florence Air and Missile Museum, Florence, SC
Grissom Air Force Base Heritage Museum, Grissom AFB, Peru, IN
Henry Ford Museum, Dearborn, MI
Henley Aerodrome and Museum of Transport, Athol, ID
Hurlburt Field Memorial Air Park, Hurlburt Field, FL
Intrepid Sea-Air-Space Museum, USS *Intrepid*, New York, NY
Langley Air Force Base Collection, Hampton, VA
Lone Star Flight Museum, Houston, TX
March Field Museum, Riverside, CA
McClellan Air Force Base, Sacramento, CA
Mud Island, Memphis, TN
Museum of Science and Industry, Chicago, IL
National Air and Space Museum, Silver Hill, MD
National Air and Space Museum, Washington, DC
New England Air Museum, Windsor Locks, CT
Ohio History of Flight, Columbus, OH
Pima Air Museum, Tucso, AZ
Planes of Fame East, Minneapolis, MN
Plattsburgh Military Museum, Plattsburgh AFB, New York, NY
Queen Mary and Spruce Goose, Los Angeles, CA
Robbins Air Force Base Museum of Aviation, Warner Robbins AFB, GA
Selfridge Military Air Museum, Selfridge ANG Base, MI
San Diego Aerospace Museum, San Diego, CA
Strategic Air Command Museum, Offut AFB, Bellville, NE
Travis Air Force Museum, Travis AFB, CA
United States Air Force Museum, Barstow, CA
United States Air Force Museum, Wright Patterson Air Force Base, Dayton, OH
United States Army Transportation Museum, Fort Eustis, VA
Virginia Aviation Museum, Ashland, VA
Wagons to Wings Museum, Morgan Hill, CA
Weeks Air Museum, Tamiami, FL
Wings of Freedom Air and Space Museum, Willow Grove, PA

CANADA

Canadian Museum of Flight, Richmond, BC
Canadian National Exhibition, Toronto ON
Canadian Warplane Heritage, Mount Hope, ON
Kingston City Council, Kingston, ON
National Aviation Museum, Richmond, BC
Royal Canadian Air Force Club, Hamilton, ON
Western Canada Aviation Museum, Winnipeg, MB

UNITED KINGDOM

Aces High, North Weald, Essex
Aerospace Museum, Cosford, Shropshire
AAEE Boscombe Down, Boscombe Down, Wiltshire
Battle of Britain Museum, Hendon, London
Bomber Command Museum, Hendon, London
Fleet Air Arm Museum, Yeovilton, Somerset
Imperial War Museum, Duxford, Cambridgeshire
Imperial War Museum, London
International Helicopter Museum, Weston-super-Mare, Avon
Midland Air Museum, Coventry, West Midlands
The Mosquito Aircraft Museum, London Colney, Herts
Museum of Science and Industry, Manchester
Plane Sailing, Duxford, Cambridgeshire
RAF Museum Collection, RAF Cosford, Shropshire
Royal Museum of Scotland — Museum Flight, East Fortune, Lothian
Science Museum, Yeovilton, Somerset
The Shuttleworth Collection, Hatfield, Herts
The Shuttleworth Collection, Old Warden, Bedfordshire
Ulster Folk and Transport Museum, Holywood, County Down, Northern Ireland
Wales Aircraft Museum, Cardiff

AUSTRALIA

Central Australian Aviation Museum, Alice Springs, NT
Royal Australian Navy Museum, Nowra, NSW
War Memorial, Griffiths, NSW

OTHER ADDRESSES:

ALBANIA

War Museum, Gjirokaster

BELGIUM

Musée Royal de L'Armée, Brussels

BRAZIL

Museu de Armas, Bebeduoro
Museu do VARIG, Porto Alegre

CHINA

Aeronautical Institute, Peking
Military Museum, Peking

CUBA

Museo de Playa Giron, Playa Giron

CZECHOSLOVAKIA

Narodni Technicke Muzeum, Prague
Technicke Muzeum v Brne, Brno

DENMARK

Dansk Veteranflysamling, Stauning

EGYPT

Cairo Museum, Cairo

FINLAND

Keski-Suomen Ilmailumuseo, Tikkakoski

FRANCE

Aero Club de la Somme, Abbeville
Aero Retro, St Rambert d'Albon
L'Amicale Jean-Baptiste Salis, La Ferte Alais
L'Armée de l'Air, Base Aerienne, Reims
Musée Aeronautique de Champagne, Brienne-le-Chateau
Musée d'Avions au Mas Palegry, Perpignan

GERMANY

Auto + Technik Museum, Sinsheim
Deusches Museum von Meisterwerken der Naturwissenschaft und Technik, Munich
Dornier GmbH, Oberpfaffenhofen
Luftfahrtausstellung, Hermeskeil
Luftwaffen Museum, Hamburg
Museum Fur Verhehr Und Technik, Gatow, Berlin
RAF Gutersloh, Gutersloh

INDIA

Indian Air Force Museum, Palam, New Delhi

INDONESIA

Armed Forces Museum, Jakarta

ISRAEL

Israeli Air Force Historical Collection, Beersheba

ITALY

Museo Nazionale dell Scienze e della Tecnica, Milan
Museo Storico dell'Aeronautica Militare Italian, Vigna di Valle

KOREA

Korean War Museum, Seoul, South Korea

MALAYSIA

Muzium Negara, Kuala Lumpur

NETHERLANDS

Aviodome, Shipol
Luchtmacht Museum, Soesterberg

NEW ZEALAND

Museum of Transport and Technology, Western Springs, Auckland

POLAND

Muzeum Lotnictwa I Astronautyki, Krakow
Muzeum Oreza Polskiego, Kolobrzeg
Muzeum Wojska Polskiego, Warsaw

SOUTH AFRICA

South African Air Force Museum, Lanseria
South African Air Force Museum, Snake Valley

SPAIN

Museo del Aire, Madrid

SWEDEN

Svedino's Bil Och Flygmuseum, Ugglarp
Flygvapenmuseum Malmer, Liknopen

SWITZERLAND

Museum der Schweizerischen Fliegertruppe, Dubendorf
Verkehrshaus der Schweiz, Lucerne

THAILAND

Royal Thai Air Force Museum, Bangkok

USSR

Air Force Museum, Monino

VIETNAM

Ba'o Tang Quan Ch'ung Khong-Quancc, Hanoi